SACRED SITES OF MINNESOTA

JOHN-BRIAN PAPROCK
TERESA PENEGUY PAPROCK

Trails Books
Black Earth, Wisconsin

Library of Congress Control Number: 2003105891
ISBN: 1-931599-26-2
Editor: Stan Stoga
Project Manager: Michael Martin
Assistant Project Manager: Erika Reise
Photos: John-Brian Paprock
Designer: Kortney Kaiser
Cover Photo: Richard Hamilton Smith

Printed in the United States of America.

08 07 06 05 04   6 5 4 3 2 1

Trails Books
A division of Trails Media Group, Inc.
P.O. Box 317 • Black Earth, WI 53515
(800) 236-8088 • e-mail: books@wistrails.com
www.trailsbooks.com

*D*EDICATION

*D*EDICATED TO OUR *F*ATHERS

Our Father in Heaven: Creator and First Person of the Holy Trinity

The Father of Waters: The Mississippi River

*Our fathers Thomas Pigneguy (Teresa's dad) and
Dr. Kenneth E. Paprock, Ph.D. (John-Brian's dad)*

*Our stepfathers Ray Nielsen, William F. Koehl (d. 1988), and
Richard E. Roderick*

*All of our spiritual fathers and teachers, especially:
H. E. Metropolitan Thomas Mar Makarios Thirumeni, our bishop;
H. E. Metropolitan Paulos Mar Gregorios (d. 1996);
Most Reverend Archbishop James Toombs (d. 1970);
and Right Reverend Bishop John Schneyder.*

NORTHERN

TWIN CITIES

SOUTHEASTERN

SOUTHWESTERN

Lake of the Woods

Rainy Lake

Namakan Lake

Rainy R.

Hallock
Roseau
Baudette

Red River

International Falls

Upper Red Lake

Thief River Falls

East Grand Forks
Crookston

Lower Red Lake

Red Lake

Lake Winnibigoshish

Ely
Embarrass

Grand Marais

Tofte

Chisholm
Hibbing

Virginia

Bemidji

Lake Itasca

Leech Lake

Grand Rapids

Two Harbors

Moorhead

Detroit Lakes

Park Rapids

Menahga

Perham

Nisswa

Wadena

Mississippi R.

Aitkin

Cloquet

Duluth

Sandstone

Pelican Rapids

Fergus Falls

Brainerd

Mille Lacs

Bois de Sioux R.

Long Prairie

Little Falls

Mora

St. Croix R.

Wheaton

Alexandria

Sauk Centre

Milaca

Pine City

Morris

St. Cloud

Ortonville

Chisago City
Anoka

Taylors Falls

Willmar

White Bear Lake
Stillwater

Madison

Litchfield

Minneapolis

St. Paul

Montevideo

Edina

Redwood Falls

New Prague

Cannon Falls

Red Wing

Lake Pepin

Wabasha

Marshall

New Ulm

St. Peter

Northfield

Rochester

Winona

Pipestone

Slayton

Mankato

Faribault

Owatonna

Mississippi R.

Luverne

Windom

Albert Lea

Lanesboro

Worthington

Fairmont

Austin

Preston

Caledonia

$\mathcal{C}$ONTENTS

$\mathscr{P}$REFACE
$\mathscr{W}$HERE DOES ONE FIND THE $\mathscr{S}$ACRED?

Ancient sites beckon you to hit the road soon.
—From a fortune cookie received by the authors before
traveling over 12,000 miles researching local sacred sites.

People have always sought out those special places where there is a strong connection with the divine. The ancient Celts referred to them as "thin places," where the veil separating Earth from the spirit world was virtually transparent. They are the places that inspire feelings of awe, of reverence, of reassurance.

Throughout history, certain geographical spaces have attracted people of a particular religion or belief system—sometimes, people of more than one religion or belief system. For example, Jews, Christians, and Muslims all consider Jerusalem a sacred city; early Christian churches were often built on land already considered sacred by other religions.

For the traveler seeking to find the spirit—however he or she chooses to define that term—Minnesota provides many opportunities. Most sacred sites simply exist quietly. There may be one right down the street from you, and you may not know of its presence. This book will help you find some of them.

When we began to list the sites for this book, we found no single resource for the information we wanted to include. We found many instances of cultural or scientific selectivity, and a lot of confusing and contradictory data.

Certainly, every person defines the concept of sacredness differently. You may have your own sacred site in your home or backyard that is yours alone. You may find someone else's beliefs strange and therefore find their sacred site hard to accept or comprehend. This book will provide locations and descriptions of sacred spaces you may want to visit—either because they reflect your own belief system or because you wish to learn about someone else's belief system. We purposely did not include the private or fragile places that we discovered during our research.

Minnesota is blessed with a large number of sacred sites, many of which are unique. We have included roughly 350 sacred sites in this book. Among those sites are retreat centers, churches, temples, cemeteries, and effigy mounds. We have included some of the oldest holy places in the state, sites that have meaning for ancient as well as modern people, as well as many more recent sites. Some of the sites have national significance. Each sacred site described in this book has one or more of the following qualities:

• It is considered sacred by a group (or groups) of people, not an individual.
• It is on the National Register of Historic Places (NRHP) or is otherwise of historic significance. Properties on the National Register must be associated with either events of broad historical significance or with the lives of persons of outstanding importance. Other elements in the evaluation of NRHP sites include distinctive characteristics of a particular architectural type or high artistic value.
• It is otherwise unique. For example, we included places that are the subject of legends, which makes them culturally significant.

If a site fit one or more of these criteria, we then rated it in four categories: historic relevance, uniqueness, aesthetic beauty, and intrinsic value (the "awe" factor). This guide represents the highest-rated sites, based on a totaling of the ratings in the four categories. Obviously, these are highly subjective rankings, but the transcendent quality of these places needed a certain subjective, perhaps spiritual, response in order for decisions to be made about inclusion in this book.

All of the sites in the book are open to the public. Some are open all the time, while others require advanced arrangements (we have included phone numbers and contacts so you can call ahead). Some can only be viewed outside, usually due to antiquity. Most of the sites can be visited for free or for a small admission. Some are in state parks, and you will need to either purchase an annual pass to all state parks or a day pass to the individual park to visit such sites.

Various rules of conduct are appropriate for certain sites. For example, some churches may require formal dress. Silence is appropriate at most sites, especially when visiting Native American effigy mounds. It is inappropriate to walk on the mounds.

A few additional guidelines apply to the traveler to all sacred places:

• When visiting a sacred site, especially if it represents a belief system different from your own, be cognizant of the reverence others have for it. Be respectful of others' beliefs about the location, even if you don't share those beliefs.
• Ask questions when appropriate: take advantage of the visit to find out something you didn't know. But be respectful of people who may be at the site to worship. Make the time to stay and ask questions when worship is concluded.
• Ask about the appropriateness of taking photographs; although most

public places do not have such restrictions, some groups consider it highly inappropriate to record certain ceremonies in any manner.

• It is always appropriate to pray or meditate quietly at any of these sites, but do not enter an altar area or touch sacred items without asking or being invited.

• Do not expect to be included in ceremonies or traditions from outside your religion or belief system, and do not engage in ceremonies not approved by the current caretakers of the site. If there is any doubt, ask.

• Most important, these are holy places, sacred to at least one group of people now or in the past. Ask yourself, "What makes this sacred?" Can you "feel" its power?

May all your journeys and pilgrimages to sacred places be fruitful, nurturing, and healing. May the "thin places" bring you closer to things divine, allowing you to catch a glimpse of the spirit worlds not normally seen.

Reverend John-Brian Paprock
Teresa Peneguy Paprock

$\mathcal{A}$CKNOWLEDGMENTS

We would like to thank God and all those who assisted in this endeavor.

We would also like to thank Christopher River-Paprock and our parents for their interest, encouragement, and support; the hosts and guardians of sites we visited, who honored us by welcoming us into their sacred spaces and taking the time to share their history and their faith with us; the agencies and local organizations that helped us compile the information we needed, no matter how obscure; and our friends and coworkers who supported us by providing suggestions, sharing ideas, and helping us stay optimistic even when the going got tough.

We debated about naming the names of many of you that remember our visit and our adventure, but realized it was likely we would forget someone important. So, to the many to whom we wanted to note here (and those we did acknowledge), please accept our deepest appreciation for all the information and assistance you provided.

God bless and keep each of you and may you be blessed tenfold the kindness you have shared.

A NOTE ABOUT THE PRESERVATION OF SACRED PLACES

Throughout our research and travels, it became clear to us that many sacred places have been desecrated or destroyed. Ignorance has played a major role in this mindless destruction. Greed has wreaked havoc on sacred places, especially where there may have been artifacts of commercial or collectible value. Fanaticism in various forms is another key motivating factor in the desecration. In addition, construction and development projects impact both the natural and the cultural landscapes. One of our sincerest hopes is that by identifying publicly accessible sites, we will instill in people a greater appreciation of diverse understandings of sacredness, and thus increase awareness, honor, and respect of sacred sites.

There are also sacred places of historic and cultural value that have been abandoned and have fallen into ruin through neglect. These may or may not have present guardians. Sometimes a simple designation of "historic" by a civil or religious authority can mean the difference between destruction and preservation.

Fortunately, laws have been written to protect sacred places, either by recognizing their historic and cultural value (through the National Register of Historic Places) or by recognizing various burial sites as private cemeteries. In addition, there are federal and state laws that protect Native American remains and artifacts, including the federal Native American Graves Protection and Repatriation Act (NAGPRA) of 1990 and Minnesota's 1978 Private Cemeteries Act. These laws require that burials are identified and that efforts are made to avoid negative effects to them prior to the initiation of any activities that could result in their destruction. These laws have severe penalties for noncompliance, including large fines and prison terms.

Section 307.08 of Minnesota's Private Cemeteries Act affords all human burial grounds and remains older than 50 years protection from unauthorized disturbance. This statute applies to burials on public and private lands or waters, and includes prehistoric Native American burial mounds as well as historic cemeteries. Under provisions of this statute, the Office of the State Archaeologist (OSA) is charged with identifying, authenticating, and protecting these burial areas. Efforts to protect burial sites emphasize "preservation-in-place," that is, maintenance of the burial area in its original location and condition.

The Minnesota Indian Affairs Council (MIAC) works with the OSA in rescuing and reburying disturbed remains in their original burial grounds, if possible. If you have any questions about sacred burial places and cemeteries, or if you notice any vandalism or other unusual disturbances, you should consult either OSA or MIAC.

We support organizations that advocate and engage in preservation efforts of sacred sites both locally and nationally. Two national agencies engage in efforts to preserve and protect sacred places, and several Minnesota-based organizations do similar work. Please support their efforts.

PARTNERS FOR SACRED PLACES is the only national nonprofit, nonsectarian organization devoted to helping congregations preserve, sustain, and actively use historic sacred places.

1700 Sansom Street, 10th Floor, Philadelphia, Pennsylvania 19103
Phone: (215) 567-3234; Fax: (215) 567-3235
www.sacredplaces.org; partners@sacredplaces.org

SACRED SITES INTERNATIONAL FOUNDATION, established in September 1990, advocates the preservation of natural sites, such as mountains, rivers, rocks, and springs, as well as human-made sacred places. The foundation believes that protecting sacred sites is key to preserving traditional cultures and time-honored values of respecting the earth. The foundation is an all-volunteer organization, governed by a Board of Directors guided by an Advisory Board of Native People and other experts in the field of site protection. Some examples of sacred sites recognized by Sacred Sites International include pilgrimage routes, petroglyphs and pictographs, burial sites, archaeological sites having sacred significance, ceremonial and calendric sites, memorials, and labyrinths.

1442A Walnut Street, #330, Berkeley, California 94709
Phone/Fax: (510) 525-1304
www.sitesaver.org; sacredsite@aol.com

THE MINNESOTA INDIAN AFFAIRS COUNCIL (MIAC) is the official liaison between state and tribal governments. The mission of the Indian Affairs Council is to protect the sovereignty of the 11 Minnesota Tribes and the well-being of Native American people throughout the state of Minnesota.

1819 Bemidji Avenue, Bemidji, Minnesota 56601
Phone: (218) 755-3825; Fax: (218) 755-3739
www.indians.state.mn.us; Joseph.Day@state.mn.us

THE OFFICE OF THE STATE ARCHAEOLOGIST (OSA) is charged with sponsoring, conducting, and directing research into the prehistoric and historic archaeology of Minnesota; protecting and preserving archaeological sites and objects; disseminating archaeological information through the publication of reports and articles; identifying, authenticating, and protecting human burial sites; reviewing and licensing archaeological fieldwork conducted within the state; and enforcing provisions of Minnesota statutes.

Mark J. Dudzik, State Archaeologist
Fort Snelling History Center, Saint Paul, Minnesota 55111-4061
Phone: (612) 725-2411; Fax: (612) 725-2427
www.admin.state.mn.us/osa

THE MINNESOTA HISTORICAL SOCIETY is a private, nonprofit educational and cultural institution established in 1849 to preserve and share Minnesota history. The society collects and preserves historical items, and tells the story of Minnesota's past, through interactive and engaging museum exhibits, extensive libraries and collections, 25 historic sites, educational programs, and book publishing.

345 West Kellogg Boulevard, Saint Paul, Minnesota 55102-1906
Phone: (651) 296-6126
www.mnhs.org

INTRODUCTION
RELIGION IN MINNESOTA

Turn to one another; love one another; respect one another;
respect Mother Earth; respect the waters—because that is life itself!
—Phil Lane, Sr. (Dakota elder)

It has been said that "wherever you go, there you are." Therefore the framework of humankind's existence—a peoples' beliefs about their relationship with the universe around them, both seen and unseen—accompanies them wherever they go, whether they are travelers, explorers, nomads, pioneers, or settlers. Newly established sacred places become intimate and familiar to them as their relationship to God and the universe is gradually revealed in their surroundings. Minnesota's early settlers saw the state's wondrous natural beauty as a sign that they were in God's country, where they could experience the fullness of life.

When people leave their homeland, either by choice or necessity, they seek out places where they can live in harmony. If the new place is agreeable, they build familiar structures to enhance their spiritual connectedness and to express their gratitude for life. As they gradually set down roots, their shrines of remembrance and gratitude become places of devotion. Cemeteries and similar sites where people have left this existence become hallowed ground, as well as reminders of a cultural and spiritual heritage.

Minnesota encompasses about 85,000 square miles of diverse habitat, from rolling hills and prairies to stark granite cliffs, from pine forests to bogs. And then there are the lakes—after all, Minnesota is "The Land of 10,000 Lakes." But even that astounding figure is an understatement: there are more than 15,000 lakes in the state. In fact, Minnesota, with 4,000 square miles of water, has the greatest water surface area of any state.

The state's rivers have played a key role in its commerce, transportation, even its geographic boundaries. A few—the Rainy in the north, the Red in the west, and the Saint Croix and Mississippi in the east—provide geographical boundaries. Minnesota is the location of the headwaters of the Mississippi, America's chief waterway and a symbol of the nation's might and energy. In the upper third of its course, the Mississippi flows through a land that has been molded by glaciations over millions of years. Some of the oldest known rock in the world has been found poking through the surface here.

Jacques de Noyon, a French Catholic explorer who arrived in far northern Minnesota in 1688, was the first European to set foot in the region. Long before he paddled the Rainy River, the Dakota had occupied the land; but even they were not the first inhabitants. Archeologists believe people appeared in the area now known as Minnesota around 9,000 B.C.E., and some early signs of human life in the area go back over 10,000 years. This evidence points to the use of pottery, as well as to the development of elaborate religious rituals and sites, in particular pictographs, petroglyphs, and burial mounds.

The Dakota were followed by the Ojibwe in the north of what is now the state of Minnesota, while the Dakota, Fox, Sac, and Ho-Chunk inhabited the south. There is some debate about which of these tribes represented the region's "original" people. Although the Dakota have the best historical claim to this title, their tribal lands over the years have become small, scattered pockets in southern Minnesota. The Ojibwe have secured the greatest amount of tribal land in the state (almost exclusively in the northern portion), and there is no doubt or confusion that it is their home, as it has been for hundreds of years. Certainly, the Ojibwe and Dakota (among others) have been calling this land home longer than any white settlers have.

The Sacred Land

According to Dakota legend, the Creator brought forth human beings from the center of the world (or the universe), which was located at the confluence of the Mississippi and Minnesota Rivers. Then humanity was saved from a catastrophic flood at the place where the Pipestone National Monument, a sacred shrine to the indigenous tribal people across North America, now stands in southwestern Minnesota. Many tribes believe the red, soft stone is a remnant of their ancestors.

Early inhabitants of Minnesota regarded numerous facets of nature as sacred. There are sacred lakes and islands throughout the state. There are sacred stones, rocks, and bluffs—some designated by symbols, both painted and carved. They express living stories, legends, mythic tales, heroic deeds, lean times, and more. It is easy to assume these are prehistoric remnants, but there is some evidence that many symbols were created when early white settlers arrived in the area. There may even be places where native symbols are being drawn to this day.

The first European immigrants and explorers recognized the area's pervasive sacredness. The first French to visit the region were traders, called voyageurs, and Catholic missionaries. The French held the region's first Christian services in the late seventeenth and early eighteenth centuries, and they erected the first chapels. These efforts were particularly evident along the North Shore of Lake Superior, the Rainy River and Boundary Waters, and the Mississippi, including the area that is now the bustling Twin Cities.

For a time under Spanish rule in what was called New France and Louisiana, the future state of Minnesota became part of the vast Northwest Territories after the Louisiana Purchase in 1803. With the acquisition of the territory by the United States, the French abandoned their forts and missions in Minnesota. In the mid-1880s, Catholic missions reemerged when German Catholics, as well as Irish and other European settlers, arrived. French Canadians, inspired by the early French missionaries, helped establish many memorials throughout the state.

Protestant missions were also very much in evidence during the 19th century. They focused primarily on the Dakota, compiling dictionaries and translating Bibles and songs into the Dakota language. One translator and missionary, Congregationalist Samuel Pond, brought his mission work to Fort Snelling, in what is now the Twin Cities area. In 1835, a Protestant mission was established at a trading post at Lac qui Parle on the Minnesota River. There, Joseph Renville, the trading post owner, and several missionaries recorded the Dakota alphabet and translated scriptural passages and hymns into the Dakota language, in addition to spreading the Christian Gospel.

In the mid-1800s, the Dakota began a series of major uprisings against white settlers throughout the upper Midwest. The uprisings resulted in bloody reprisals from the settlers and the eventual expulsion of the Dakota to reservations scattered throughout the area. In this vacuum, newly arriving European settlers established towns, especially in southern Minnesota, and with them, various places of worship. Many of the newcomers hoped that railroad lines would be built close to their towns and villages, thereby increasing commerce and trade. By the end of the 19th century and early into the 20th, the settlers abandoned many of these towns and villages when the railroads laid track leading elsewhere. Many inhabitants moved to thriving commercial centers in search of better opportunities. Some of their places of worship fell into disrepair and eventually disappeared. Others survive, maintained by descendents of those early pioneers.

Many of these churches were progressive and Protestant, usually established by the area's growing population of Scandinavians, who embraced freedom of thought and expression. Some of these remained isolated, while others merged and joined with churches of a similar mind. With sparse populations in many areas of the state, interdenominational mergers and other cooperative efforts became fairly common. Sometimes such mergers resulted in churches with complicated histories of denominational affiliation, often including several name changes. Some of these early cooperative efforts would much later become part of the ecumenical movement. A progressive religious attitude continues to this day throughout much of Minnesota.

In the early 20th century, many Slavic immigrants settled in Minnesota, primarily in the northeast where jobs in the lumber industry and iron mines were plentiful. These settlers established some of the earliest Eastern Orthodox and Catholic churches in the Midwest. The oldest Russian Orthodox Church in America is in the Twin Cities. In addition, settlers created the earliest Jewish synagogues in the state around this time.

By the 20th century, the cities of Minneapolis and Saint Paul had become a powerful and vibrant urban center. They continue to be a magnet for diversity and growth. Eight of Minnesota's 10 largest cities are in the Twin Cities area. Well over half of the state's population lives within 20 miles of the Dakota's "center of the world"—where the Mississippi meets the Minnesota River, south of downtown Saint Paul.

Minnesota is well known as a place of both physical and spiritual healing. Rochester's Mayo Clinic complex started with the Franciscan Sisters working with Dr. Mayo. The mineral springs of Owatonna and Mankato were well known to Native Americans and early settlers. And the Hazelden Foundation, a world-renowned alcohol and drug abuse treatment facility and publishing house north of the Twin Cities, is one of the premier places for 12-Step recovery from all forms of addiction. It is said that there are more 12-Step recovery meetings per person in the Twin Cities than in any other metropolitan area in the United States.

In the 1960s, people from the Middle and Far East became the newest immigrants to Minnesota. Bringing along their rich cultural and spiritual heritage, these newcomers have established religious centers, mosques, and temples to enhance their own spiritual connectedness with this new place and to express gratitude for the chance to achieve a new life. Buddhists, Muslims, Hindus, and others have brought their faith and their hopes to the New World.

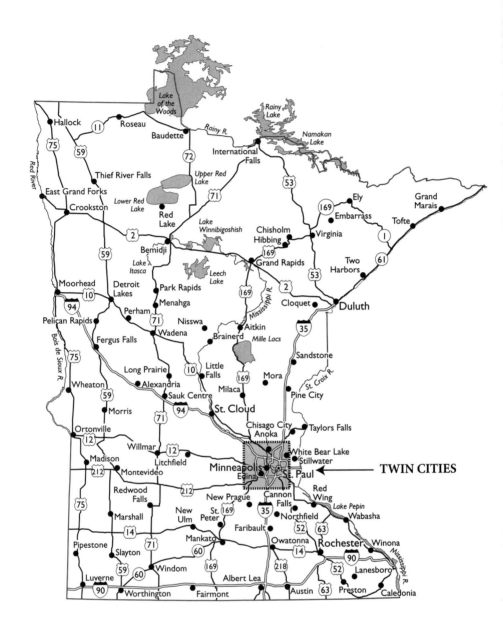

TWIN CITIES

Including the counties of Anoka, Carver (eastern portion),
Dakota (northern portion), Hennepin, Ramsey, Scott (northern portion),
and Washington (western portion)

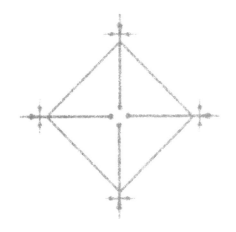

CHAPTER 1
TWIN CITIES AREA

Where the Falls of Minnehaha
Flash and gleam among the oak trees,
Laugh and leap into the valley. . . .
—Longfellow, "Song of Hiawatha" (1855)

Pig's Eye, converted, thou shalt be like Saul
Arise; and be, henceforth—Saint Paul.
—Minnesota Pioneer (region's first newspaper)
when Saint Paul, formerly Pig's Eye,
became the territorial capitol

Some people may not realize that the "Center of the World" is in the Twin Cities, where Pike Island juts out from the place where the Mississippi and the Minnesota Rivers merge. The Dakota named the site Taku Wakan Tipi (interpreted by various sources to mean "The Dwelling Place of the Gods" or "The Center of the World"). The spot is sacred to the tribe. The Twin Cities area is of immense importance to the people of Minnesota; more than half of the people in the state live there, and eight of Minnesota's 10 largest cities are in the Metro. Pike Island, which sits at the confluence of the Mississippi and Minnesota Rivers, was named for the famous explorer Zebulon Pike; today, it is part of Fort Snelling State Park.

To early Native Americans, whose spiritual beliefs formed the fabric of their lives, it was strange that some whites were religious and some were not. But Father Louis Hennepin, like other white missionaries, was motivated by his faith to explore the new world, and he spent time exploring the area that would become the Twin Cities. In addition to spreading the word of Christianity, the missionaries engaged in farming, writing, and compiling translation dictionaries for Native American languages, among other endeavors. In studying the culture of the tribes in the region, these early missionaries learned of the Native American belief in a Great Spirit but also in a variety of gods for other needs and occasions.

In the 19th century, Methodists, Congregationalists, Episcopalians, Quakers, Universalists, and Presbyterians came to the Twin Cities area from New England. Each new wave of pioneering immigrants—Germans, Irish, Poles, Swedes, and Norwegians, among others—brought new religious traditions. Jews from western Europe settled in Minneapolis in the late 1870s and founded a synagogue. Five decades later, there were 280 organized religious congregations in Minnesota; today there are more than 52 denominations and representatives of all world religions to be found in the Twin Cities alone.

Best of the Twin Cities

- **Adath Jeshurun Synagogue**, Minnetonka (striking contemporary architecture that conveys the congregation's rich traditions)
- **Basilica of Saint Mary**, Minneapolis (breathtaking size, with nearly 700 images of angels throughout)
- **Beth El Synagogue**, Saint Louis Park (large, modern structure full of symbols)
- **Cathedral of Saint Paul**, Saint Paul (gigantic, with numerous small chapels and beautiful statues)
- **Hennepin Avenue United Methodist Church**, Minneapolis (beautiful and impressive structure)
- **Indian Mounds Park**, Saint Paul (large, well-preserved mounds)
- **Lakewood Cemetery and Chapel**, Minneapolis (several impressive and religiously diverse monuments in the cemetery; stunning chapel)
- **Minnesota Zen Center**, Minneapolis (peaceful meditation center with a Japanese-style garden)
- **Normandale Japanese Garden**, Bloomington (traditional Zen garden)
- **Saint Constantine Ukrainian Catholic Church**, Minneapolis (beautiful mosaic domes)
- **Saint Katherine Ukrainian Orthodox Church**, Arden Hills (traditional yet modern design)
- **Saint Maron Catholic Church**, Minneapolis (one of the oldest Catholic Maronite congregations in the Midwest; the Saint Maron shrine garden)
- **Saint Mary's Orthodox Cathedral**, Minneapolis (first Russian Orthodox church in lower 48 states)
- **Catholic Church of Saint Peter**, Mendota (faithfully preserved structure built in 1853)
- **Taku Wakan Tipi at Coldwater Spring**, Minneapolis ("the center of the world" for the Dakota nation)
- **Temple Israel**, Minneapolis (home of Minneapolis's first Jewish congregation)

NATIVE AMERICAN SITES

Taku Wakan Tipi at Coldwater Spring

For the Dakota, Taku Wakan Tipi, a spot marked by four ancient oak trees, was a place for sacred prayer, used for ceremonies and burial rites. The site was also said to be the home of the powerful god of the waters and the underworld. A spring provided the Dakota with medicine water, and they believed that nearby Pike Island was the place where humankind first emerged. The spot was of special importance, because, as explorer Joseph M. Nicollet put it, "The Mdewakanton [Dakota] people considered the mouth of the Minnesota River to be the middle of all things—the exact center of the earth."

For white pioneers, the area would become a settlement, a military post, and trading post. A small hill that now overlooks the Fort Snelling prairie between the Veterans Administration Hospital and the Naval Air Station was called Morgan's Bluff in pioneer times. A tunnel led from the hill to the Minnesota River.

Taku Wakan Tipi was considered the center of the world for the Dakota. The sacred site came close to destruction in 2000, when a highway was to be built nearby; environmental studies showed the water runoff from the highway would have destroyed the spring. An outcry from area residents, based on historical and spiritual reasons as well as hydrological ones, prevented the project from being completed. On May 14, 2001, a large celebration and ceremony with people from all faiths was held to bless the spring. On that day, said Chris Leith, Dakota spiritual elder, "All four colors of people came together. When we all come together like this in peace, there will be no room for the racists." Now, representatives from the Mendota Mdewakanton Dakota Community are planning an interpretive center to tell the story of their sacred place. The Friends of Coldwater are trying to prevent pedestrian/bicycle trails from interfering with the comtemplative nature of the site.

Nearby, the Minnehaha Creek flows for 20 miles. The waterfall on the creek is one of the area's oldest and best-known tourist attractions. This small waterfall, with its ripples and rapids beneath, seems to laugh—hence its name, Minnehaha ("laughing water" or "curling water"). Near the top is a life-sized bronze statue of the famed Hiawatha carrying Minnehaha over the stream. The falls were made famous by Henry Wadsworth Longfellow's poem "Song of Hiawatha," written in 1855.

The five-mile Minnehaha Trail starts from the Fort Snelling State Park steamboat landing. A wide part of the trail, called the South Minnehaha Addition, was the site along the Mississippi River where the Fifth U.S. Infantry had a tent camp while constructing Fort Snelling. They called it Camp Coldwater because of the huge volumes of cold water that flowed from the valley-side springs. Another part of the trail reaches the Lower Glen, which has a historical marker. There is a foot trail between this spot and the gorge where the falls are. The Dakota would hide from enemies in the Lower Glen.

The area is seen as a place of peace, where Dakota people and European settlers worked together to understand each other. The majority of the ancestors of the Mendota Mdewakanton Dakota Community can be traced back to the area around Mendota, just across the river, in the 1700s. Today they meet monthly at the Mendota VFW "to share precious knowledge with future generations so they may also know their past, enjoy their present, and preserve their Dakota future."

The Acadia Memorial Cemetery sits on Pilot Knob, the highest point in Mendota. This was also the site of the treaty of Mendota.

Minnehaha Falls and Park is located on Minnehaha Parkway at Hiawatha Avenue (Highway 55), Minneapolis. For information write to the Minneapolis Park and Recreation Board, 250 South Fourth Street, Minneapolis, MN 55415; (612) 348-2243. Acadia Memorial Cemetery is on Highway 13, west of Highway 55, in Mendota (Dakota County). To reach Coldwater Spring from Highway 55, turn east at the 54th Street light and then quickly turn south on the new frontage road. Go one block to the Bureau of Mines front gate. Go through the gate and continue heading south one more block. Watch for the historical marker and the pond on the right.

Saint Anthony Falls

Before being named Saint Anthony Falls by Father Louis Hennepin in 1680, the site had been a sacred meeting place for Dakota, Sac, Fox, and Ojibwe, and the 40-foot falls (known as Owah Menah, "falling waters") have many legends attached to them. Owanktayhee, the mammoth and Dakota god of water, had his home in these waterfalls and another in Morgan's Bluff at Fort Snelling. According to Dakota legend, the wife of Anpetu Sapa (Dakota for "dark day") committed suicide at the waterfall here with her infant son when she discovered her husband had taken a second wife. She took their son and paddled to a small island in the center of the river, dressed in her bridal garments and head of eagle feathers; their infant son dressed as a warrior. She then paddled for the falls, singing her death song. On the shore her husband heard the chant, raced from his new wife's side, and tried to call her back, but it was too late. The canoe rushed over the falls. The Dakota say her spirit, like a Madonna, rises with foam resting lightly on the waters, holding her infant to her bosom. She would look upon the prairies where she once lived happily and then disappear into the falls. A display next to the falls shows many unusual and large prehistoric fossils that have been found there. (See Saint Anthony Falls in the "Catholic Sites" section later in this chapter.)

Saint Anthony Falls is located in downtown Minneapolis.

Indian Mounds Park

A group of 18 tall mounds survive here, an impressive collection when compared to the mounds of many other midwestern sites. When traveling back from the West, the Dakota would bring the bones of the dead with them and bury them here. Unusual finds in the area include a skull encased in red clay and the skull of a five-year-old child. The mounds once covered the entire bluff that overlooks the Mississippi River, according to explorer Jonathan Carver, but many have been destroyed since the 1850s when the settlers began coming into the area. Until the early 1900s, settlers looted and vandalized the mounds under the guise of exploration.

Located at Mounds Boulevard and Earl Street, two miles south of
downtown Saint Paul.
www.fromsitetostory.org/tcm/21ra0010indianmp/21ra0010indianmp.asp

Wakon-teebe (Carver's Cave)

The Dakotas called this cave Wakon-teebe, "The House of Spirits," after some explorers of the tribe reported seeing flickering lights inside. The Mdewakanton called it "The Dwelling of the Great Spirit." Nineteenth-century explorers discovered the cave and reported on the "hieroglyphics" (petroglyphs) that they found inside. Sketches of the glyphs by Robert Sweeny in 1867 are on display at the Minnesota Historical Society. The cave would eventually be named after Captain Jonathan Carver, a Connecticut native who explored the cave. He was one of the first white men to publish data about a cave in North America. "I found (the cave) to be a great curiosity," he wrote. "I found many strange hieroglyphics cut in the stone some of which were very ancient and grown over with moss. On this stone I marked the arms of the king of England." Although the meaning of the glyphs remains a mystery, it is assumed that they represented spiritual concepts. (For more on rock drawings, see chapter 4.)

Because of a nearby railroad, the cave structure was endangered and the entrance became covered. It was forgotten until 1913 when J. H. Colwell of the Dayton's Bluff Commercial Club and others raised funds and relocated the cave mouth with the aid of a horse-drawn scraper. Thereafter, the cave provided an exploring place for local children and a shelter for homeless people during the Great Depression. The entrance was covered with debris again, and the cave remained blocked until 1977, when the Saint Paul Community Services Division opened it briefly for inspection.

A historical marker for the cave can be found on Mounds Boulevard between
Cherry and Plum Streets, Saint Paul.

Lake Minnetonka

The Dakota kept Lake Minnetonka a secret for years, as they believed it was the spiritual home of Manitou, the Great Spirit. The lake has more than 110 miles of shoreline and is 27 miles long. U.S. soldiers "discovered" the lake in 1822 but kept it a secret from their superiors. When the state mapped the area in 1853, the lake turned out to be much larger than had been previously thought. Its name comes from the Dakota words mine ("water") and tonka ("big"). Within Lake Minnetonka, Enchanted Island is a traditional site for many Native American ceremonies.

Lake Minnetonka is located in western Hennepin County. Enchanted Island is reached via the Zimmerman Pass Bridge from Tuxedo Boulevard in Shorewood.

What's in a Name?

• **THE CITY OF MOUND**, situated on Lake Minnetonka, was named after the burial mounds in the area. Over the years, some people have believed the mounds were left by the Lost Tribes of Israel; others believed they were from a Mongolian tribe.

White Bear Lake

The town of White Bear Lake was founded in 1858, named after the spirit of a sacred white bear who lived in the lake. In his book *Life on the Mississippi*, Mark Twain referred to it as "a lovely sheet of water." Walking trails with interpretive signs and information about legends are available. Native Americans believed White Bear Lake had healing powers.

For a brochure, contact the White Bear Historical Society, 4735 Lake Avenue, White Bear Lake, MN 55110; (651) 426-0479.

Mound Springs Park

Mound Springs Park harbors a group of burial mounds that are part of the Bloomington Ferry Mound Group. Set on a bluff overlooking the Minnesota River, more than 1,000 mounds from the Late Woodland Indian culture are thought to be in this group, estimated to be between about 300 and 1,200 years old. Most of them, however, have not been identified and are on private property. Twenty or so are in Mound Springs Park and are thus accessible.

Located at the far eastern end of East 102nd Street, a few blocks south of Old Shakopee Road in Bloomington; (952) 563-8877.

Chaska Indian Burial Mounds

A few Indian burial mounds can be found in the middle of the village of Chaska, which also boasts a 19th-century business district and central square with a wooden bandstand.

Chaska is located on Highway 212 in Carver County.

Dakota Burial Mounds

These conical burial mounds, estimated to be over 2,000 years old, are located in Veterans Memorial Park in Shakopee. An informational plaque marks the site.

Located off Highway 101 along the Minnesota River on the east side of Shakopee in Scott County.

Peninsula Point

The spot where the Rum River joins the Mississippi also marks the historic meeting place of many Native Americans, including the Dakota and Ojibwe. The preserved area, at Peninsula Point Park in the town of Anoka, is also the location of the Father Hennepin Stone *(see the Father Hennepin Stone description under Catholic Sites for directions to the park).*

Peninsula Point Park, Anoka

*C*ATHOLIC *S*ITES
Churches and Related Sites

Father Hennepin Stone

There is some question as to whether Father Louis Hennepin inscribed his name on a stone in Anoka's Peninsula Point Park. However, the stone is there, and many believe that he carved it himself to commemorate the first Catholic Mass in the Twin Cities.

In Anoka, take the frontage road from the bridge on Sauk Prairie Street, off Highway 169, to the mouth of the Rum River.

Saint Anthony Falls

Father Louis Hennepin, a Belgian Franciscan missionary, was sent to this area by King Louis XIV of France to do missionary work. In 1680, as a captive of the Dakota, he became the first white person to see what he would name Saint Anthony Falls (after his patron saint, Saint Anthony of Padua). The falls are the most abrupt drop in the Mississippi River (72 feet over the distance of a mile) and the only true falls on the river.

The priest would eventually be rescued by the French explorer Daniel Graysolon du Lhut. When Father Hennepin returned to Europe he wrote a book, first published in 1683, which described the falls and the Mississippi.

Visitors can take a 1.8-mile self-guided tour along the banks of the Mississippi River, crossing at the 1883 Stone Arch Bridge (right below the falls) and the Hennepin Avenue Bridge. Brochures are available through the Saint Anthony Falls Interpretive Center, 125 East Main Street, Minneapolis, MN 55414; (612) 627-5433.

Our Lady of Lourdes Catholic Church

In 1680 near the spot where Our Lady of Lourdes Catholic Church now stands, Father Louis Hennepin first sighted and named Saint Anthony Falls. Using limestone quarried on nearby Nicollet Island, construction began on this building in 1856. It was originally a Universalist Church, and the Universalist Society of Saint Anthony used it until 1877. Today, located in downtown Minneapolis, it is the oldest continuously used church in the city. A French Catholic congregation purchased the building and renamed it Our Lady of Lourdes, the first church in the county to be so named. The structure was enlarged in 1881 to accommodate the growing parish. The church has maintained its French identity. A plaque in the front entry reads, "In commemoration of the courageous French explorers whose discoveries inspired French settlement and anticipated the growth of the City of Minneapolis."

Located at One Lourdes Place, Minneapolis; (612) 379-2259; www.ourladyoflourdes.com

Chapel of Saint Paul

We may have the Chapel of Saint Paul to thank for the city of the same name becoming a large metropolitan area. In 1849, Bishop Mathias Loras of Dubuque, Iowa, sent Father Lucian Galtier to the Twin Cities area as a missionary. The Chapel of Saint Paul was erected in 1841, the first church building for white settlers in Minnesota. At that time, the area was known as Pig's Eye, after Pierre Parrant, its first settler. The chapel became the focus of the growing town—and eventually the town was renamed after it. In 1851, the chapel was abandoned for the Catholic Church of Saint Peter, which was being built across the river in Mendota. Today, Galtier Plaza, a glitzy shopping, business, and condominium complex in downtown Saint Paul, is named for Father Galtier. The high-rise buildings of the complex stand in stark contrast to the original chapel that the priest described as "so poor that it would well remind of the stable at Bethlehem."

A historical marker can be found at the location of the original chapel at Kellogg Boulevard and Minnesota Street in Saint Paul.

Church of Saint Peter

Except for some minor remodeling, this 35-by-75-foot limestone church looks exactly as it did when it was completed in 1853. It sits on a hill immediately south of the Sibley House historic park at the confluence of the Minnesota and Mississippi Rivers. The main church building nearby is newer and larger, and the school next door has historical articles and photographs. Services are still held regularly in the old church.

Located at 1405 Highway 13, Mendota; (651) 456-0646; www.stpetersmendota.org; church@stpetersmendota.org

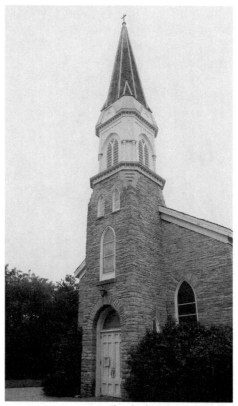

Church of Saint Peter, Mendota

Church of Saint Mary of the Purification

The parish Church of Saint Mary was founded in 1865 by French and Irish immigrants. Almost immediately afterward, the church building was erected with locally made brick. Reverend Anatole Oster helped finance the construction through a parish festival, which took in $700. He also established a Total Abstinence Society in 1876 with the help of Father John Ireland, who would later become the first archbishop of Saint Paul.

9

After Father Oster left the parish, the pastors of Saint Mark's parish served Saint Mary's until 1878, when Reverend John J. Slevin was appointed resident pastor. Over the past century, the church building has seen a number of improvements, including the addition of stained glass windows, an ornate altar, a steeple, vestibule, and new front steps. The structure is on the National Register of Historic Places.

Located at 15850 Marystown Road, Shakopee, Scott County; (952) 445-3469.

Basilica of Saint Mary, Minneapolis

Basilica of Saint Mary

The Basilica of Saint Mary in Minneapolis, the first basilica built in America, is one of two principal cathedrals, along with the Cathedral of Saint Paul, for the Saint Paul/Minneapolis Archdiocese. Although the first mass was held here in 1914, the building was not completed until 1929. Today the church prides itself on its welcoming spirit: "Within these traditional stone walls lies a warm and open community. We are more than your local parish. We are more than the impressive building downtown. We are a group of people who have come together in a beautiful, spirit-filled place who live our faith everyday by how we interact with those around us." The basilica is the spiritual home of 3,400 households, more than half of which are young adults.

The church was built under the direction of Archbishop John Ireland. It is an excellent example of French architecture. Inside, there are 675 images of angels, done in glass, marble, steel, bronze, plaster, and wood. The exterior of the building is almost as long as a football field, and the distance to the apex of the dome is nearly as long. Other highlights include the recently restored Rose Window, the coat of arms especially designed for this basilica, and a carved in situ crucifixion tableau modeled after a miraculous crucifix of Lympias, Spain.

Emmanuel Masqueray, chief architect for the 1904 Saint Louis World's Fair and the Cathedral of Saint Paul (see below), designed the basilica in 1906. The side chapel, Mary Chapel, contains a statue from the founding church, established in 1876. In the front garden is a copper statue by Fred Slifer, dedicated to Father Louis Hennepin.

Located at 88 17th Street North (between Hennepin and Laurel Avenues), Minneapolis; (612) 333-1381; www.mary.org; bsm@mary.org; call ahead for tours.

Cathedral of Saint Paul

The second cathedral of the Saint Paul/Minneapolis Archdiocese was modeled after Saint Peter's Basilica in Rome, under the direction of Archbishop John Ireland, known as Minnesota's greatest churchman. Designed by Emmanuel Masqueray (see above), the French Baroque building was completed in 1915 and can seat more than 3,000 worshippers.

The columns and chapels surrounding the sanctuary are made of various imported marbles. Six chapels are dedicated to the patron saints of the ethnic groups that settled the area: Saint Anthony for the Italians; Saint John the Baptist for the French Canadians; Saint Patrick for the Irish; Saint Boniface for the Germans; Saints Cyril and Methodius for the Slavs; and Saint Therese of Lisieux for the missionaries.

Large statues of the four evangelists (Matthew, Mark, Luke, and John) can be found in the niches of the four main tiers of the church. Charles Connick designed the rose windows and the other smaller windows. Many inscriptions are carved in the stone on the interior walls and on the facade of the front of the building. Five large bells cast in France were added to the church in 1987. The Shrine of Nations is of special interest.

The building is more than 306 feet high, 307 feet long, and 216 feet wide. Twenty-four stained-glass windows depicting heavenly choirs are set into the huge copper dome. Four 25-foot mosaics by Michaelangelo Bedini represent Justice, Prudence, Temperance, and Fortitude. The cathedral also features two historic frescoes—one in honor of French native Joseph Cretin, first bishop of Saint Paul, and the other depicting the opening of the cathedral by Archbishop Ireland.

A half-hour video, part of a tour, tells more of the church's history and of the early days of Saint Paul. Guided tours are held Monday, Wednesday, and Friday at 1 p.m. The church is open for visitors Monday–Tuesday and Thursday–Saturday, 8 a.m.–6 p.m., Wednesday, 8 a.m.–4 p.m., Sunday, 1–6 p.m.

Located at 1840 Summit Avenue and 239 Selby Avenue, Saint Paul; (651) 228-1766; www.archspm.org/html/cathedral.html; www.cathedralsaintpaul.org

Assumption Catholic Church

Founded in 1854, this was the first German Catholic parish in Minnesota. Its soaring 210-foot twin towers with iron crosses are Saint Paul landmarks. The Romanesque Revival structure, built of local limestone, was completed in 1873. It was modeled after the Ludwigskirche in Munich, Germany. When it was built, many people thought it was too plain for Victorian tastes. The interior features intricate carvings and paintings. The church is on the National Register of Historic Places.

At 51 West Ninth Street (between Saint Peter Street and Saint Joseph Lane), Saint Paul; (651) 224-7536. Tours available by appointment.

Chapel of Saint Thomas Aquinas

This building is an adaptation of the Byzantine style used for basilicas in several northern Italian cities during the Renaissance; the building's shape is based on the Latin cross. The first celebration in the chapel took place during the feast of Saint Thomas Aquinas in 1918.

Located on the campus of the University of Saint Thomas, Saint Paul; (651) 962-6578; mcklein@stthomas.edu

Saint Martin's-by-the-Lake Church

Major George Camp had this tiny chapel built in 1887 for the wedding of his daughter, whose wedding gown train was too long for his house. Cass Gilbert designed the chapel.

Located along Lafayette Bay on Lake Minnetonka in Wayzata.

Our Lady of Victory Chapel

The chapel, built in 1924 at the College of Saint Catherine in Saint Paul, was inspired by Saint Trophine at Arles in Provence, France. The Sisters of Saint Joseph of Carondelet, who operate the 110-acre campus, established the college. Approximately 3,900 are enrolled in the women's college, which is open for retreats from June to August. A traditional English garden has stood at the west end of campus since the 1920s, and the outdoor grass labyrinth is always open to the public. In addition, the college's Carondelet Center also runs the Wisdom Ways Resource Center for Spirituality.

The center is located at 1890 Randolph Avenue, the college and chapel at 2004 Randolph Avenue (between Fairview Avenue South and Cleveland Avenue South), Saint Paul; (651) 696-2750 or (651) 690-6000; www.stkate.edu

Saint Genevieve of Paris Church

The area north of the Twin Cities in which this parish developed is known as the French Section. The parish was founded in 1853, and the first building was built in 1854, the first of four that were to occupy this site. Goiffon Road in Centerville is named after Joseph Goiffon, the pioneer missionary from France who served as the church's rector from 1861 to 1881. He named the church to honor a beloved French saint.

Located in Anoka County at 7087 Goiffon Way, Centerville; (651) 429-7937.

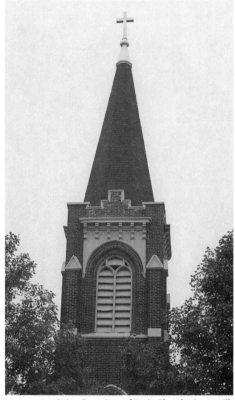

Saint Genevieve of Paris Church, Centerville

Church of Saint Agnes

Bohemian immigrants designed and built this shrine church to Saint Agnes in 1887; it is on the National Register of Historic Places.

Located at 105 Lafon Lane North (at Kent Street), Saint Paul; www.stagnes.net

Saint John the Evangelist Church

One of the first churches in the Twin Cities area, Saint John the Evangelist Church dates back to 1851. The church is on the National Register of Historic Places.

Located just north of Saint Paul at 380 Little Canada Road East, Little Canada; (651) 484-2708.

Epiphany Fatima Shrine

This unique and beautiful rosary garden, on the grounds of the Church of the Epiphany, features a beautiful Stations of the Cross, a series of bas-reliefs of Mary, a waterfall, and a shrine.

Located at 11001 Hanson Boulevard NW, Coon Rapids; (763) 755-1020; www.epiphanymn.org

Epiphany Fatima Shrine, Coon Rapids

Retreat and Religious Centers

Benedictine Meditation Center
of Saint Paul's Monastery

With its invitation to "listen with the ear of your heart" and to firmly plant one's actions in the teachings of Christ, the Benedictine Meditation Center "offers a way, amidst the often chaotic demands of everyday life, to find balance between leisure and work. Never lofty or complex, Benedictine prayer is quiet and meditative, with few words. It prepares one for the challenges and the joys of life in communion with others and nature." People of any religious background are invited to meditate there on Saturday mornings. Located in downtown Saint Paul, the Meditation Center is connected to the Benedictine Center of Saint Paul's Monastery, as a ministry of the Sisters of Saint Benedict. At another location, the Benedictine Center offers retreat space to individuals and groups.

The Meditation Center is located at 68 West Exchange Street, Saint Paul. The Retreat Center is located at 2675 Larpenteur Avenue East, Saint Paul; (651) 224-6261; www.osb.org/spm/bencenter.html

A few additional Catholic retreat centers reside in the Twin Cities area:

Convent of the Visitation

2455 Visitation Drive, Mendota Heights; (651) 683-1700; wisdom@vischool.org; www.visitationsisters.org; www.visitationsisters.com

Dunrovin, Christian Brothers Retreat Center

15525 Saint Croix Trail North (Highway 95), Marine-on-St-Croix; www.dunrovin.org; dunrovinCBRC@juno.com

Jesuit Retreat House

8243 De Montreville Trail North, Lake Elmo; (651) 777-1311.

Grounds at the Jesuit Retreat House, Lake Elmo

Loyola Spiritual Retreat Center - Spiritual Renewal Resource

389 North Oxford Street, Saint Paul; (651) 641-0008; http://loyolasrr.org; Staff@Loyolasrr.org

Eastern Rite Catholic Churches

Saint Constantine Ukrainian Catholic Church

A Ukrainian landmark, this church was constructed in 1972, replacing the original structure built in 1913. It is topped with five onion domes spaced in the shape of a cross, in the Ukrainian tradition. The interior is richly decorated with icons and mosaics, and the main dome is covered with 7,000 blue, gold, white, black, and red tiles. The iconography is similar to that of Saint Sophia's Cathedral in Kiev, Ukraine. The church is part of the Ukrainian Catholic Eparchy of Saint Nicholas of Chicago. Saint Constantine's is located one block from Saint Michael's Ukrainian Orthodox Church, and the Ukrainian Orthodox Church of St George's is also nearby.

Located at 515 University Avenue NE, Minneapolis; (612) 379-2394.

Saint Maron Catholic Church

This beautiful golden-domed church has a statue of Saint Maron in the garden. The original Maronite congregation, composed of Lebanese immigrants, was established in 1903. Since then, the group has worshipped in several different locations, including its recently built church. It is part of the Eparchy of Our Lady of Lebanon of Los Angeles.

Located at 219 Sixth Avenue NE, Minneapolis; (612) 379-2758;
www.eparchyla.org; another Maronite church is Holy Family,
203 East Robie Street, Saint Paul; (612) 291-1116.

Saint Maron Catholic Church, Minneapolis

$\mathcal{E}$ASTERN $\mathcal{O}$RTHODOX $\mathcal{S}$ITES

Orthodox Christian Sites

The Orthodox Church dates back to the earliest days of Christianity and has remained virtually unchanged since its founding. Although there are fewer Orthodox Christians in the United States than Catholics or Protestants, millions of Orthodox believers practice their religion worldwide, mostly in eastern European, African, and Asian countries. There are two branches of Orthodoxy—Eastern Orthodoxy (Greek, Romanian, Russian, etc.) and Oriental Orthodoxy (Coptic, Armenian, etc.). Art and architecture are extremely important to Orthodox Christians; symbolism is a big part of their faith. Icons, or "windows into heaven," are highly revered. Almost all of the Orthodox Christians in Minnesota are in the Twin Cities and can be traced to the waves of immigration from eastern Europe at the end of the 19th and the beginning of the 20th century.

Saint Mary's Orthodox Cathedral

Russian immigrants from central Europe founded the congregation in 1887, and they built the church one year later. It was the first Russian Orthodox church in the continental United States. In 1907, the church's first priest, Father Alexis Toth, was canonized.

Located at 1701 NE Fifth Street, Minneapolis; (612) 781-7667; www.stmarysoca.org; a Russian Orthodox chapel associated with the church is located at Lakewood Cemetery (described later in this chapter).

Saint Mary's Romanian Orthodox Church

Another historic Saint Paul landmark, this house of worship is modeled after the church of Sanicolaul Mare in Romania. Built in 1913, Saint Mary's contains archives and old books of church liturgies, as well as a beautiful carved iconostasis and altar.

Located at 854 Woodbridge Street, Saint Paul; (651) 488-5669.

Saint Michael's Ukrainian Orthodox Church

By the early 1920s, a number of Ukrainians had settled in the Twin Cities. The Ukrainian National Home was established in Minneapolis in 1923, and two years later, plans began for a church. With the blessing of the Most Reverend Archbishop John Theodorovich, Saint Michael's Ukrainian Orthodox Church was founded. The church is one block from Saint Constantine Ukrainian Catholic Church, and the Ukrainian Orthodox Church of St. George's is also nearby.

Located at 1925 505 Fourth Street NE, Minneapolis; (612) 379-2695.

Saint Michael's Ukrainian Orthodox Church,
Minneapolis

Saint Katherine's Ukrainian Orthodox Church

This Ukrainian baroque church is in the style of 17th-century Ukrainian architecture. The design combines Byzantine and Baroque elements. Saint Katherine's was inspired by the Cathedral of Saint Sophia in Kiev and the church buildings of Kiev Pecherska (Cave) Lavra Monasteries, both in Ukraine. Parishioners created the iconostasis. The building contains about 4,000 square feet, including a landscaped plaza, narthex, choir area, and crying room for mothers with infants, and can accommodate about 200 worshippers. It is 90 feet to the top of the cross on the central cupola. Exterior materials are white stucco with precast art-stone trim. The cupolas of the church and the roofs of the parish hall are standing seam copper, and the interior design makes good use of natural light.

Located at 1600 Highway 96 West, Arden Hills; (651) 636-0206 or (651) 697-1995.

Saint Mary's Greek Orthodox Church

This church is laid out in the shape of a cross, with the vertical axis extending from the back of the church to the Royal Doors (the iconostasis), representing the creation of light and darkness. The congregation dates back to the late 1890s, and the current building was erected in 1957 on the spot where the first Christian missionaries settled in Minneapolis. Like all Orthodox churches, the church faces east, to remind the worshipper of Christ, the light of the world. Centered over the cross is the dome that contains an icon of Christ Pantocrator (Greek for "all-powerful" or "almighty"), with his hand in blessing. On the east wall behind the altar is the Platyter, the icon of Theotokos (Mary the Mother of God).

The icon screen separates the altar from the center of the church. To the left is Theotokos with the Christ child and to the right is an icon of Christ. There is an icon of the Last Supper above the Royal Doors.

Located at 3450 Irving Avenue South, Minneapolis;
(612) 825-9595; www.stmarysgoc.org

Saint Mary's Greek Orthodox Church

Ethiopian Orthodox Tewahedo Church of Our Savior

This church is located in a converted Lutheran church, established by the local Ethiopian community in 1994. The church's interior is traditionally Ethiopian, with Ethiopian-style iconography and a golden iconostasis.

Located at 4401 Minnehaha Avenue South, Minneapolis; (612) 721-1222.

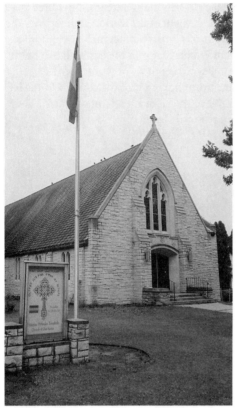

Ethiopian Orthodox Tewahedo Church of Our Savior

Saint Mary's Coptic Orthodox Church of Minnesota

The Coptic Church is the ancient church of the See of Alexandria. Most Copts are Egyptian or Middle Eastern. This church was established in 1963, making it one of the earliest Coptic Orthodox churches in the country. While the outside of the church has not yet been renovated, a stunning iconostasis stands inside.

Located at 501 Sixth Avenue South, South Saint Paul; (651) 455-8947; www.geocities.com/copticorthodoxchurch

Saint Sahag Armenian Orthodox Church

In 301 C.E., Armenia became the first nation to declare Christianity as its national religion. The first Armenian immigrants to Minnesota date back to 1899, and Saint Sahag was their first church in the Twin Cities area. In 2000, their descendants took a former Protestant church and refurbished it in the Armenian tradition. Minneapolis architect Francius Bilbulian donated his time to convert the 90-year-old building. The first Armenian service was held on January 15, 2001, and the church was formally consecrated by Archbishop

Khajag Barsamian in 2002. He anointed all the brass crosses and all the arches. Above the altar, the church's most notable feature is an icon of Mary with the child Jesus, which was written locally (in Orthodoxy, icons are "written" rather than painted). Monthly services are held for Armenians from the Dakotas to western Wisconsin.

Located at 203 North Howell Street, Saint Paul; (651) 686-0710.

EPISCOPAL SITES

Church of Gethsemane

With a cornerstone laid in 1883, this is the oldest church building in Minneapolis. It is in the same spot as the original 1856 log church. The church, considered the Mother Church of the Episcopal Diocese of Minnesota, has started 26 other Episcopal churches, two hospitals, and an orphanage. Gethsemane's bell was the first church bell rung in Minneapolis. The church features a beautiful series of stained glass windows depicting Christ praying in the garden of Gethsemane. The structure is on the National Register of Historic Places.

Located at 901–905 Fourth Avenue South (at Ninth Street South), Minneapolis; (612) 332-5407.

Saint Mark's Cathedral

This Episcopal congregation was established in 1852, and parishioners completed the building in 1908. The Diocese of Minnesota designated it a cathedral in 1941. The large Gothic Revival castle is filled with museum-quality art.

Located at Loring Park near the heart of downtown, 519 Oak Grove Street (at Hennepin Avenue), Minneapolis; (612) 870-7800; www.st-marks-cathedral.org

The Labyrinth

The labyrinth is an ancient mystical tool that has recently come back into vogue. The labyrinth is similar to a maze, except that it has only one narrow path, made up of 11 concentric circles with a 12th in the center. There are 34 turns on the path going into the center, and there is no "wrong" path. Each number of each element in the labyrinth has symbolic religious significance. The rose shape in the center is universally recognized as a symbol for enlightenment.

The earliest known labyrinth tied to Christian history can be found in a fourth-century basilica in Algeria where the words "Santa Ecclesia"

("Holy Church") are at the labyrinth's center. During the twelfth century, when wars made it too dangerous for Christians to make pilgrimages to Jerusalem, seven European cathedrals were assigned to be places of pilgrimage. Many of these cathedrals had labyrinths embedded in the floor, which signaled the end of the journey. The cathedral in Chartres, France, has one of the best examples of this kind of labyrinth.

Today, labyrinths can be indoors or outdoors, portable or permanent, made of grass or carpet or stone. A person enters into a meditative state while walking along the winding path (about a third of a mile long). Although most labyrinths are found at Catholic and Episcopal sites, the labyrinth is an ecumenical and interfaith tool that people of all faiths can utilize.

The Villa Maria Retreat Center in Frontenac, Minnesota, welcomes visitors to its labyrinth with these words: "May your sacred walk be a source of discovery, of insight, of solace, of healing. Above all may it be a sacred pilgrimage, a pilgrim's journey."

Permanent labyrinths in the Twin Cities area can be found at the following locations:

- **CARONDELET CENTER** (grass),
1890 Randolph Avenue, Saint Paul; (651) 690-8830.
- **TRINITY HOSPITAL** (painted concrete),
3410 213th Street West, Farmington; (651) 460-1169.
- **SPIRIT OF LIFE PRESBYTERIAN CHURCH** (grass),
14401 Pilot Knob Road, Apple Valley; (952) 423-2212.
- **UNITY CHURCH** (painted concrete),
9025 Tamarack Road, Woodbury; (651) 731-5440.
- **CHRIST EPISCOPAL CHURCH** (grass),
7305 Afton Road, Woodbury; (651) 735-8790.
- **OUR LADY OF THE LAKE CHURCH AND CEMETERY** (grass),
2385 Commerce Boulevard, Mound; (952) 472-1284.
- **OUR LADY OF VICTORY CHAPEL** (grass),
1890 Randolph Avenue, Saint Paul; (651) 690-6000.

Trinity Church

Built in 1862 in Excelsior, this is the oldest Episcopal church building in Minnesota still in use. The missionary Bishop Jackson Kemper consecrated the original log church. The structure is on the National Register of Historic Places.
Located at 322 Second Street, Excelsior; (952) 474-5263.

*L*UTHERAN *S*ITES

Norway Lutheran Church/The Old Muskego Church

This 1843 building was the first Lutheran church built by Norwegians in America. It was constructed in Wisconsin and then moved to its current site, at the Luther Northwestern Theological Seminary in Saint Paul, in 1904. Today, no religious services are held here, but the historic church is open to visitors. An explanatory plaque is located at the seminary entrance.

Located at 2375/2481 Como Avenue West (between Luther Place and Hendon Avenue), Saint Paul; (612) 641-3456.

Central Lutheran Church

Once known as Mount Olivet Lutheran Church, this gigantic church in Minneapolis, which seats more than 2,500 people, was completed in 1928. It is the largest Lutheran church in North America. The stone building has French and English Gothic elements, with windows exported from England that are similar to those at Westminster Abbey. The organ has 5,781 pipes and 78 speaking stops. Two smaller chapels are used for weddings and baptisms.

Located at 333 12th Street South, between Fourth Avenue South and Clinton Avenue, Minneapolis; (612) 870-4416.

Lutheran Brotherhood Collection of Religious Art

Christian art by European and American masters from the 15th to the 20th century is on display here. There are a few paintings, over 90 drawings, and more than 400 prints, including etchings, engravings, woodcuts, and lithographs. Many of the pieces of art are circulated to Lutheran churches, seminaries, and colleges. "The goal of the collection is to have religious art of highest quality by world's most renown artists of all nations and periods."

Located at 625 Fourth Avenue South (across Fourth Avenue from the Government Center), Minneapolis; (612) 340-7000. Open Monday through Friday from 10 a.m. to 4 p.m.

Christ Church Lutheran

This 1949 church is so unique that it is already on the National Register of Historic Places. Designed by Finnish-American architect, Eliel Saarinen, this was the last architectural project completed before his death. The structure features a unique Gothic style, with no parallel surfaces, resulting in a design that is deceptively simplistic and deeply spiritual. With a seating capacity of 600, the building also boasts of some of the finest acoustics of any church in the United States.

Located at 3244 34th Avenue South, Minneapolis; (612) 721-6611.

PRESBYTERIAN SITES

Samuel Pond Missions

Samuel Pond established several early missions in what is today the Twin Cities area. In 1834, with the permission of the local Indian agent stationed at Fort Snelling, he and his brother Gideon, Presbyterian missionaries from Connecticut, began to minister to a band of Dakota on the eastern shore of Lake Calhoun.

There, the missionaries worked with Chief Cloud Man to teach new farming techniques to the Dakota. In 1840, Samuel became the minister at Fort Snelling; and, in 1849, his brother reorganized the ministry as the Oak Grove Presbyterian Church in Bloomington. In addition to his ministerial work with the Dakota, Samuel Pond became a student of the native language, creating the first Dakota-English dictionary in 1852.

In 1880, resorts were built along Lake Calhoun, and one has since become Saint Mary's Greek Orthodox Church (see previous listing), at the very spot of Samuel Pond's mission.

In 1847, Pond's missionary work continued across the Minnesota River in Shakopee. There he established a Presbyterian mission for the local band of Dakota. He also built a residence in which he lived until his death in 1891. Pond was instrumental in establishing Shakopee's first Presbyterian congregation in 1855. A historical marker stands at the site of what was the original mission.

The historical marker is located just off Cavanaugh Drive in Shakopee, Scott County.

Crane Island

In the early part of the 20th century, Bethlehem Presbyterian Church in Minneapolis founded a retreat on Crane Island in Lake Minnetonka. In 1906, 25 families, who were members of the church, founded the Crane Island Association led by Charles E. Woodward, the association established a summer community of Christian families "away from the noise and confusion of the city." By 1915, a total of 15 family cottages and a caretaker's cottage had been built. Middle-class residents of a variety of occupations lived there, taking a ferry to and from the island. The well-preserved cottages are one-and-one-half to two stories high and are of frame construction with clapboard siding. Fourteen of the extant cottages are on the National Register of Historic Places.

Located on the western end of Lake Minnetonka.

House of Hope Presbyterian Church

This is one of the country's best examples of the Gothic Revival style. Originally the first private home on Summit Avenue, the limestone villa has arched windows and a crenellated bell tower. The building was renovated in the 1970s when the neighborhood was designated a historic district.

Located at 797 Summit Avenue, Saint Paul.

Westminster Presbyterian Church

Modern glass office buildings today surround this Gothic structure, built in 1897 and now on the National Register of Historic Places. The church, which seats about 1,500, has one of the 25 largest Presbyterian congregations in the nation. The structure features a red interior with an in-the-round altar. There is a small Gothic side chapel with stained glass, most of it from the Henry Willet studio in Philadelphia. The stained glass at a side window is rumored to be from the Tiffany studios. Tours are available by appointment. The exterior is graced by the "Birth of Freedom," an eighteen-and-one-half-foot sculpture created by local artist Paul Granlund.

Located at 1201 Nicollet Mall (83 12th Street South), Minneapolis; (612) 332-3421.

First Presbyterian Church

Organized in 1855, this is the oldest congregation in Shakopee. The building was built in 1900 and today serves a Spanish-speaking community.

Located at 909 Marshall Road (at Shakopee Avenue), Shakopee; (952) 445-3562.

$\mathcal{B}$APTIST $\mathcal{S}$ITES

First Baptist Church, Saint Paul

Saint Paul's First Baptist Church has a long history in the community, with its roots going back to the 1840s when Harriet Bishop established a Baptist school in the area. In 1849, a church was established, with the present edifice completed in 1875. At the time, it was the largest church in Saint Paul—and likely one of the most expensive. For years, the church was the center of the area's Baptist community and gave rise to several other Baptist congregations. The church's large Gothic-style stained-glass window features the trefoil, symbolizing the Trinity, and the quatrefoil, symbolizing the four Gospel writers. The structure is on the National Register of Historic Places.

Located at 499 Wacouta Street, Saint Paul; (651) 222-0718; www.firstbaptiststpaul.org; office@firstbaptiststpaul.org

First Baptist Church, Minneapolis

The present First Baptist Church in Minneapolis, the third building housing the congregation, was erected in 1885 and is on the National Register of Historic Places. In 1853, E. W. Cressey of the American Baptist Home Missionary Society helped establish the church as the first "regular Baptist church" in the Minnesota Territory west of the Mississippi.

Located at 1021 Hennepin Avenue, Minneapolis; (612) 332-3651; www.fbcminneapolis.org

Redeemer Missionary Baptist Church

This church, founded in 1909 , formerly the Stewart Memorial Presbyterian Church, is on the National Register of Historic Places, being one of the very few churches designed in the true Prairie School style. Designed by William Gray Purcell, a protégé of Frank Lloyd Wright, the structure is much as it was when it was built, even though major renovations were completed in 2000.

Located at 116 East 32nd Street, Minneapolis; (612) 823-1081.

$\mathscr{M}$ETHODIST $\mathscr{S}$ITES

Hennepin Avenue United Methodist Church

Modeled upon Ely Cathedral near Cambridge, England, this building was erected in 1914 and seats 1,000. The exterior gray Bedford sandstone is topped by an illuminated 24-story spire, and Albert Conmick designed the stained glass.

The upstairs gallery houses one of the largest collections of religious art owned by a church in the United States; the holdings range from the 16th through the 19th centuries. The original collection was donated by lumber baron Thomas Barlow Walker. It has since grown, and several works have been restored. The church also has a labyrinth.

In 1957 the congregation merged with an all-black church, Border Methodist Church. The baptismal font is from Border Church.

Located at 511 Groveland Avenue (at Lyndale Avenue South), Minneapolis;
(612) 871-5303; www.themethodistchurch.org; tours are given on Sunday afternoons.

Scottish Rite Cathedral

The Scottish Rite Cathedral, formerly known as Fowler Methodist Episcopal Church, was erected in 1906 and features columns of rough-cut pink jasper and 13 arch stones made of polished jasper from Jasper, Minnesota. The Franklin Avenue façade has a 24-foot rose window with two faces of Christ and two scenes from the life of Bishop Charles Fowler, a Methodist missionary at this site. The Scottish Rite Bodies, a fraternal benevolent organization that is part of Freemasonry, bought the building in 1916 when the Fowler Methodist congregation merged with the Hennepin Avenue United Methodist Church. The structure is on the National Register of Historic Places.

Located at 2011 Dupont Avenue South (between 22nd Street West and
Franklin Avenue West), Minneapolis; (612) 871-1500.

Wesley United Methodist Church

In 1852, the first Methodist congregation west of the Mississippi formed, and the group built a modest church on the present site of Wesley United Methodist Church. The current building, erected in 1891, boasts a huge auditorium with a ceiling containing an impressive circular domed light. It features skylights and 32 stained-glass windows fashioned by the Tiffany Studios. The rounded pews give worshippers a close and unimpeded view of the altar and pulpit.

Located at 101 East Grant Street, Minneapolis; (612) 871-3585; www.thewesleychurch.org

*O*THER *C*HRISTIAN *S*ITES

Emerson Monument

Joseph Emerson, an early settler, inscribed 2,500 words from the Bible, along with his personal philosophy, on a monument and erected it in the city cemetery in Anoka. He died only a year later.

Located in the Anoka City Cemetery, Anoka.

Lakewood Cemetery and Chapel

Founded in the 1870s, Lakewood Cemetery, in the center of Minneapolis, is a mix of amazing architecture and sculpture. Architect Adolph Strauch created a layout of nine memorial gardens—each with a different central monument or chapel. A granite pagoda marks a Chinese section. The Lowry-Goodrich Mausoleum, the cemetery's largest monument, is a replica of the Parthenon, while the large Praying Hands Monument is another interesting structure.

The stunning Lakewood Chapel was built in 1910 and is on the National Register of Historic Places. Minneapolis architect Henry W. Jones modeled it after the Hagia Sophia (the Christian temple of Emperor Justinian I in Constantinople, which is now the principal mosque in Istanbul). The solid bronze doors are embellished with ancient religious symbols. The interior was designed by New York architect Charles Lamb; he modeled the mosaics on those of the San Marco Cathedral in Venice, Italy. The ceiling contains more than 10 million pieces of mosaic tiles that, together, depict the images of 12 angels. The 65-foot-high chapel dome is ringed with 24 stained-glass windows that serve as a sundial.

The Pool of Reflections is surrounded by trees and formal gardens; it connects the chapel with the Lakewood Memorial Community Mausoleum and Columbarium. In addition to the cemetery grounds and the individual, sometimes unique gravestones and markers, there are many other more secular monuments and places of interest. One noteworthy attraction is a chapel associated with Saint Mary's Orthodox Cathedral (described previously in this chapter).

Located at 3600 Hennepin Avenue, (between Kings Highway and the William Berry Parkway), Minneapolis.

Fort Snelling Memorial Chapel

When it was established in the early 19th century, the original chapel at Fort Snelling was the first Protestant house of worship in Minnesota. Services were held in various buildings here until 1924, when the existing chapel was built. It honors the memory of all members of the armed forces. The chapel was almost demolished in 1946 when the military post was deactivated, but various patrons kept it from the wrecking ball. Finally, the Minnesota Council of Churches set up a foundation in 1966 that advocated for its preservation. The effort was successful, and today nondenominational services are celebrated every Sunday.

According to promotional materials, more than 80 memorials are to be found in the chapel. One is a stained glass bearing the coat of arms of the Third U.S. Infantry (the oldest in the army), whose base was at Fort Snelling. Many flags that were carried by Minnesotans in battle are on display. Several stained-glass windows honor pioneer leaders and churchmen, including Samuel Pond, who came to the fort in 1834 as a missionary to the Dakota. The marble baptismal font is a memorial to Elizabeth Snelling, daughter of Colonel Josiah Snelling, who designed the fort and was its commandant from 1820 to 1824.

Located at Fort Snelling State Park, Highway 5 and Post Road, Saint Paul; (612) 725-2390; fsmc@spacestar.net; the chapel foundation is located at 1 Federal Drive, Fort Snelling, Saint Paul; (612) 970-7866; www.forministry.com/55455FSMC

Fort Snelling Memorial Chapel, St. Paul

Mormon Temple

Located in Oakdale, this is the only temple of the Church of Jesus Christ of Latter Day Saints between Chicago and Denver. The 11,000-square-foot facility, completed in 1999, serves members in Iowa, North Dakota, South Dakota, and Minnesota. The temple has several rooms, including the endowment room, the sealing room, and the celestial room (which includes a baptistery), as well as numerous paintings and murals (some over 20 feet tall) that reflect the life and teachings of the savior. The baptismal font rests upon 12 oxen representing the 12 tribes of Israel. As is the case with all Mormon temples, only members of the Mormon Church "who are living high moral standards and Christian principles" are allowed inside. A card signed by the local ecclesiastical leader certifying personal worthiness must be presented at the front desk.

Located at 2150 Hadley Avenue North, Oakdale; (651) 748-5910.

Mormon Temple, Oakdale

Minneapolis Friends Meeting House

On May 12, 1851, members of the William and Catherine Wales family became the first Quakers to settle in Minneapolis. A few years later, they organized regular meetings for the purpose of worship and prayer. In 1860, the Society of Friends built a meetinghouse at 8th Street and Hennepin Avenue in Minneapolis. The members now meet in at a location in the southern part of the city.

Located at 4401 York Avenue South at West 44th Street, Minneapolis; (612) 926-6159; mplsfriends@mtn.org

Christos Center for Spiritual Formation

This ecumenical retreat center, run by the Evangelical Lutheran Church in America, encourages the "spiritual quest through historic Christian traditions of prayer, meditation and spiritual direction. . . . It is a place to come away to solitude and silence." It is located on 51 acres of wooded wetlands just 25 minutes north of the Twin Cities.

Located at 1212 Holly Drive, Lino Lakes; (651) 653-8207; www.christoscenter.org; christoscenter@worldnet.att.net

Virginia Street Swedenborgian Church

In view of the great Cathedral of Saint Paul, this beautiful green-and-brown wooden building designed by Cass Gilbert (see the sidebar on Cass Gilbert churches in chapter 4) is on the National Register of Historic Places and is a local landmark. The Swedenborgian Church follows the teachings of Emmanuel Swedenborg, a 17th-century scientist and mystic. The Swedenborgian Church, or the Church of the New Jerusalem, promotes utopian ideas of humanism based on a belief in the essential goodness of humankind. In the 19th century, church members were active in many social reform movements. One of the most famous Swedenborgians was John Chapman, better known as Johnny Appleseed, who distributed Swedenborgian publications as well as apple seeds to areas of the Midwest. Ralph Waldo Emerson was greatly influenced by Swedenborg's philosophy, and Swedenborgian Helen Keller wrote about her beliefs in *My Religion*.

Located at 170 Virginia Street, Saint Paul; (651) 244-4553.

Minneapolis Friends Meeting House, Minneapolis

Zoar Moravian Church

This church, built in Greek Revival style, has remained virtually unaltered since it was erected by immigrants from Hopedale, Pennsylvania, in 1863, although the steeple was moved forward in 1908 to form a bell tower. It's on the National Register of Historic Places. Nearby, another historic Moravian site is the Laketown Moravian Brethren's Church, also known as Lake Auburn Moravian Church, built in 1878 in Victoria. (See more about Moravian churches in chapter 2.)

Zoar Moravian Church is located on County Highway 10, Chaska.

Virginia Street Swedenborgian, St. Paul

JEWISH SITES

Adath Jeshurun Synagogue

The oldest affiliate of the United Synagogue of Conservative Judaism west of Chicago, yet one of the newest synagogues, Adath Jeshurun is a progressive community dedicated to Torah (learning and tradition), Avodah (reverential service), and Gemilut Hasadim (acts of loving kindness).

The 75,000-square-foot domed building was completed in 1995 and houses the congregation's religious services, social events, education programs, and administrative functions. It serves 1,200 members. Although the building is contemporary, its major architectural elements reflect the congregation's history and help realize its mission. The use of stone throughout the spaces for prayer and learning represent Jewish history and the generations of the congregation. Three indoor arches at the entrance to the Grand Foyer recall Adath's former synagogue and the three "pillars" of the congregation's mission.

The first word of the Torah, B'reshit, meaning "in the beginning," is inscribed at the top of the window on the right side of the Bimah wall and the ark. The last word of the Torah, Yisrael, meaning "Israel," is inscribed at the bottom of the window to the left of the Bimah. The doors to the ark contain the Torah scrolls and are inscribed with the words to the "Shirat Hayam," the song that the Israelites sang after crossing the Red Sea on their way out of slavery. The inscription above the ark on the Bimah wall reads, U'fros aleinu sukkat sh'lomekha ("Spread over us the shelter of your peace").

Located at 10500 West Hillside Lane, Minnetonka; (952) 545-2424; www.adathjeshurun.org; office@adathjeshurun.org

B'nai Emet Synagogue

B'nai Emet Synagogue is a Conservative Jewish congregation, affiliated with the United Synagogue of Conservative Judaism. B'nai Emet was created in 1972 with the merger of three congregations—B'nai Abraham, Mikro Kodesh, and Tifereth B'nai Jacob. The current building was erected in 1974. It houses the Fingerhut Sanctuary, Baratz Social Hall, Fox Family Chapel, Goldberg Lounge, Hellman Library, Burton Education Wing, and Diana Chazin Levitt Playground.

According to promotional materials, Congregation B'nai Abraham originated in 1889 and served Jewish-Romanian immigrants in the area. Its first home, at 15th Avenue South between 3rd and 4th Streets, was a temple that seated about 300 worshipers and was packed every Saturday morning and afternoon. The second building, B'nai Abraham's home for 36 years, was located at 825 13th Avenue South. In the late 1940s and early 1950s, many of the members left the old Minneapolis neighborhood and moved to the suburbs. From 1946 to 1956, only about 10 families carried on the traditions at the old synagogue. At the same time, the Saint Louis Park B'nai B'rith began to hold meetings to meet the needs of the area's growing Jewish population. In the mid-1950s, the congregation purchased two adjacent houses where the present synagogue now stands in Saint Louis Park. The structures originally housed a chapel, congregational office, and classrooms.

Located at 3115 Ottawa Avenue South (northeast of the junction of Highway 25 and Highway 100), Saint Louis Park; (952) 927-7309; www.bnaiemet.org; info@bnaiemet.org

Bet Shalom Congregation

Bet Shalom, which means "our home" in Hebrew, was formed in 1981 as a small, warm, welcoming reform congregation. The building's architecture combines contemporary styling with features of old eastern European synagogues, with its natural woods, translucent glass, warm natural colors, and stone finishing reminiscent of Jerusalem stone. The design includes Jewish symbols and features that recall the traditional synagogue architecture, from the ark to the copper dome on the outside of the building.

The city of Minnetonka offered to change the name of the one block of Park Valley Road that borders the temple's property, requesting only that the name be "easy to pronounce." The temple is now located at Orchard and Shalom Roads.

Located at 13613 Orchard Road, Minnetonka; (952) 933-8525 or
(952) 933-3238; www.betshalom.org

Beth El Synagogue

This Conservative Jewish synagogue serves 1,350 households. The congregation goes back to 1920 when a group of young people began to meet on Friday nights in the Talmud Torah in Minneapolis to hold modern, meaningful services. They soon formed the Young People's Synagogue, with A. M. Heller of the Talmud Torah serving as rabbi. The group soon outgrew the space and purchased a house and lot on 14th and Penn Avenue North, where daily services were held. The cornerstone for a new building on that site was laid in 1925. In the early 1960s, the congregation erected a youth and activities building in Saint Louis Park, followed by a new synagogue on the site in 1968.

Visitors will first see the impressive stained-glass window depicting Jacob's dream at Beth El. Other windows depict celebrations and observances of the Jewish calendar. The Spiegel Sanctuary houses the many Sefrei Torah. Over the ark are the words, Emet, Dien, Shalom ("Truth, Justice, Peace").

Located at 5224 West 26th Street, Saint Louis Park;
(952) 920-3512 or (952) 920-8755; www.bethelsynagogue.org

Beth El Synagogue, Saint Louis Park

Beth Jacob Congregation

This congregation dates back over a century but was formally founded in 1985. Its 375 families embrace the principles of Conservative Judaism: Torah (study), Avodah (reverential service), and Gemilut Hasadim (acts of loving kindness).

Located at 1179 Victoria Curve, Mendota Heights; (651) 452-2226; www.beth-jacob.org; bjcadmin@beth-jacob.org

Kenesseth Israel Congregation

This congregation refers to itself as "the Modern Orthodox Jewish congregation of suburban Minneapolis." The congregation, formed in 1880, has about 120 families and strives to provide "a welcoming environment for Jews of all observance levels."

Located at 4330 West 28th Street, Saint Louis Park; (952) 920-2183 or (952) 920-2184; www.kenessethisrael.org

Mount Zion Temple

Established in 1855, this is Minnesota's oldest Jewish congregation. The synagogue of the present Reform congregation was built in 1955, the fourth structure in 150 years. It was designed by world-renowned architect Eric Mendelsohn and recently renovated. The unique Torah mantles have needlework depicting the four seasons, and the Hebrew lettering on the wall represents the Ten Commandments. A light burns at all times in front of the Holy Ark, representing the eternal light at the ancient Temple in Jerusalem. The Hebrew letter "Shin," similar to a "W" and a symbol of one of the Hebrew words for God, is an artistic theme in the sanctuary.

Located at 1300 Summit Avenue, Saint Paul; (651) 698-3881; www.mzion.org; mountzion@mzion.org

Shir Tikvah Congregation

This Reform congregation was formed to provide a "spirit of liberal Judaism that would welcome and encourage the participation of individuals and families of varying Jewish lifestyles." More than 100 people attended the first informational meeting in 1988. The Shir Tikvah ("Song of Hope") congregation moved into its current building in 1994 and has 275 members.

Shir Tikvah is currently affiliated with the Union of American Hebrew Congregations, the national umbrella organization for Reform congregations.

Located at 5000 Girard Avenue South, Minneapolis; (612) 822-1440; www.shirtikvah.net; office@shirtikvah.net

Temple Israel

This Reform congregation formed in 1878 as Congregation Shaarai Tov ("Gates of Goodness"); it was Minneapolis's first Jewish congregation. The synagogue is now known as Temple Israel and serves 5,000 congregants. The 23 founding members started out by renting a hall at Nicollet Avenue and Washington Avenue for Friday night worship services. They built their first synagogue two years later, a small, Moorish-style wooden building at Fifth Street and Marquette Avenue. The ladies society of the congregation helped new immigrants and the poor, cared for the sick, and prepared the dead for burial; they also sponsored lectures, recitals, dances, dinners, and bazaars to raise money for a new synagogue.

Shaarai Tov members moved their building to the corner of 10th Street and Fifth Avenue South in 1888. That building burned down in 1902, and the congregation—still small—built a stone synagogue on the site for $18,000. In the late 1920s the growing congregation, then known as Temple Israel, built a new building, which still stands today. The pillared facade reflects the Greek influence on early Judaism. The building features a design rich with symbolism: Five doors represent the five books of the Torah; 12 columns in the sanctuary signify the 12 tribes of ancient Israel; acanthus leaves in the organ grilles are a reminder of the Jews' suffering as slaves in Egypt, and the windows are dedicated to the Creation, the Patriarchs, Exodus, the Temple, the Prophets, and post-biblical ideals of one world and one humanity.

The synagogue seats 1,000 people in its sanctuary. The first building of worship with an acoustic tile ceiling (a new invention at the time), the acoustics are still so good that the Saint Paul Chamber Orchestra performs at Temple Israel on occasion.

Located at 2324 Emerson Avenue South, Minneapolis; (612) 377-8680; www.templeisrael.com; info@templeisrael.com; the tree-lined Temple Israel Memorial Park is located at Third Avenue South and 42nd Street. The chapel there is on the National Historic Register.

Temple of Aaron Synagogue

Following the ancient tradition of the building of the original Temple in Jerusalem, the main sanctuary of the Conservative Temple of Aaron Synagogue is constructed entirely of wood and brick. Its upward sweeping beams meet in an arch dominated by a star. The pillars beside the arc represent the columns named Yahin and Boaz that flanked the throne of Solomon, and, as in Solomon's Temple, they support the building's structure. Spiritually, they symbolize ethics and ritual, "the pillars of our daily lives."

There are seven short steps to the twin pulpits. Rabbis conduct services and deliver sermons from one, and the other is used by the cantor and serves as the stand from which the Torah is read.

The Ark Curtain is handwoven in authentic biblical tradition, the design includes a cloud ("For I appear in the cloud upon the Ark-cover which is upon the Ark"), wings ("And the cherubim shall spread their wings on high, screening the Ark cover with their wings"), and two trumpets ("And the Lord spoke unto Moses saying: Make thee two trumpets of silver, of beaten work shalt thou make them; and they shall be unto thee for the calling of the congregation").

The main ark is the prominent feature of the building, containing two tiers of Torahs. Two golden points at the summit represent the Cherubim that mounted the biblical Ark. The ark itself is buttressed and flanked by Israeli marble, which symbolizes ties with Israel. There are ten stained-glass windows based on the theme "the lifetime of a Jew." Outside is a beautiful sculpture garden.

A cybertour is available on-line.

Located at 616 South Mississippi River Boulevard, Saint Paul;
(651) 698-8874; www.templeofaaron.org; webmaster@templeofaaron.org

ℬUDDIST ℬITES

Minnesota Zen Center

The Minnesota Zen Center was formed in 1972 when the founding head teacher, Dainin Katagiri Roshi (1928–90), was invited to come from California to teach a small but growing group of Minneapolis students interested in Zen Buddhism. The organization's chief meditation practice center is Ganshoji, located on the shores of Lake Calhoun in Minneapolis. The center also owns and operates a retreat center called Hokyoji in southern Minnesota near the Iowa border, a facility that is in the process of renovation (see separate listing in chapter 2).

Located at 3343 East Calhoun Parkway, Minneapolis; (612) 822-5313;
www.mnzencenter.org; info@mnzencenter.org or mnzenctr@aol.com

Dharma Field Zen Center

Started in 1989, the Dharma Field Zen Center is a community dedicated to learning and sharing the teachings and practice of Zen Buddhism in a setting not bound to any one culture. The tradition of Japanese Zen is practiced.

Located at 3118 West 49th Street (at York Avenue), Minneapolis;
(612) 928-4868; www.dharmafield.org; dfield@dharmafield.org

Dharma Field Zen Center, Minneapolis

Other Buddhist centers in the Twin Cities area include:

Chua Phat An Buddhist Temple (Vietnamese),

475 Minnesota Avenue, Roseville; (651) 482-7990.

Gyuto Wheel of Dharma Monastery (Tibetan),

4011 Polk Street NE, Columbia Heights; (763) 789-4478.

Wat Lao Minneapolis (Laotian),

1429 NE Second Street, Minneapolis; (612) 789-9382.

Clouds in Water Zen Center (American),

308 Prince Street, Saint Paul; (651) 222-6968; www.cloudsinwater.org

Karma Thegsum Choling Meditation Center (Tibetan),

4301 Morningside Road, Minneapolis; (952) 926-5048.

*I*SLAMIC *S*ITES

Islamic Center of Minnesota

Islamic people of all backgrounds come to this center for worship, cultural programs, exhibits, and other activities.
Located at 1401 Gardena Avenue NE, Fridley; (763) 571-5604; www.myicm.org

Other area mosques include:

Masjid Al-Rahman,

8910 Old Cedar Road, Bloomington; (952) 883-0044.

Masjid Al-Salaam,

1460 Skillman Avenue, Maplewood; (651) 748-7688.

Masjid An-Nur,

1729 Lyndale Avenue North, Minneapolis; (612) 521-1749.

Masjid At-Taqwa,

804 University Avenue, Saint Paul; (651) 292-9675.

*H*INDU *S*ITES

Hindu Mandir

This temple is the site of the Hindu Mandir Society of Minnesota, the oldest and the largest East Indian social and religious organization in the state. The center is a converted Protestant church. The Jain Center of Minnesota uses the Hindu Mandir building for special ceremonies and events and a private residence for other services.
Hindu Mandir is located at 1835 Polk Street NE, Minneapolis; (612) 788-1751; Contact the Jain Center at (612) 937-849; www.members.tripod.com/~jaincenter

Dhyana Mandiram Ashram

This yoga and meditation center is in a Ukrainian neighborhood, with three Ukrainian churches nearby.
Located at 631 University Avenue, Minneapolis; (612) 379-2386.

Geeta Ashram Minnesota

This ashram was founded in 1972 by His Holiness Sri Swami Hari Har Ji Maharaj. It is currently being renovated and expanded.

Located at 10537 Noble Avenue North, Brooklyn Park, Minneapolis; (763) 493-4229; www.geetaashram.org

$\mathscr{U}$NITARIAN/ $\mathscr{U}$NIVERSALIST $\mathscr{S}$ITES

First Universalist Society of Minneapolis

The First Universalist Society of Minneapolis was founded in 1859. In 1992, the congregation bought the former Adath Jeshurun Synagogue building. The exterior of the building has been left unchanged because it is on the National Register of Historic Places. There are Unitarian Universalist Chalice flags flying out front. Inside is a 36-foot canvas labyrinth.

Located at 3400 Dupont Avenue South, Minneapolis; (612) 825-1701; www.firstuniv.org; firstuniversalist@firstuniv.org

First Universalist Society of Minneapolis, Minneapolis

First Unitarian Society of Minneapolis

Founded in 1881, the First Unitarian Society of Minneapolis is located up the hill from the Guthrie Theater.

Located at 900 Mount Curve Avenue, Minneapolis; (612) 377-6608; www.unitarian.org/fus; uufus@unitarian.org

OTHER SITES

Gurudwara

The Sikh Society of Minnesota converted a commercial building into this gurudwara. Services are held on Sundays.

Located at 5831 University Avenue NE, Fridley; (612) 574-0886; www.mnsikhs.com; mnsikhs@hotmail.com

Normandale Japanese Garden

Both Shinto and Zen principles are at work in this cultural garden, featuring a soothing blend of water, rock, and vegetation. It is a place of quiet and refreshment of the spirit. Japanese hold gardens in great reverence and often put them next to religious shrines and temples. Upon entering, the visitor will see a large granite pagoda lantern to the right. In the middle of the pond lies a hexagonal Shinto shrine called a bentendo, with curved roof and copper bells, a symbol of good luck, beauty, and music. A zigzag bridge protects against evil spirits, because it is believed that they can only travel in straight lines. The garden is open sunrise to sunset, June 1–September 30, unless a wedding is in progress. Guided group tours are available by appointment.

Located next to Normandale Community College, 9700 France Avenue South; (952) 487-8145.

Peace Bridge at Lake Harriet Rock Garden

The Peace Bridge features a stone from "ground zero" in Nagasaki, one of the two Japanese cites that were leveled by atomic bombs at the end of World War II. On the stone is inscribed the words "May Peace Prevail on Earth," in Japanese, English, Russian, and Spanish. Hideaki Tsutsumi, a victim of the bomb, donated the stone.

Built in 1985, this traditional Japanese bridge also features a Peace Pole given by the Society for World Peace in Chiba, Japan, and dedicated by Mayor Hitosi Motoshima of Nagasaki on his way to a United Nations nuclear disarmament meeting. Each year on August 6, the anniversary of the bombing of Hiroshima, the Women's International League for Peace and Freedom holds a memorial service here.

Just a short walk from the rock garden is the wonderful Lake Harriet Rose Garden; both are part of the Hennepin Park System.

Located on northeast corner of Lake Harriet on Roseway Road, in southwest Minneapolis; (612) 661-4806.

Lake Harriet Spiritual Community, Minneapolis

Lake Harriet Spiritual Community

This spiritual organization offers an alternative to traditional religion by honoring all spiritual paths. The community's church is also used by a variety of local groups, including the Spirit of Life Spiritualist Church (part of the National Spiritualist Association); groups that celebrate the full and new moon and sacred earth rituals; a synergy meditation circle; and psychic and alternative health practitioners, among others.

The domed church dates from the early 20th century and once housed the Church of Spiritual Science, a now defunct denomination, and the former Lake Harriet Community Church.

4401 Upton Avenue South, Minneapolis; (612) 922-4272; www.lhcc-mn.org

Temple of ECK®

This is the headquarters of Eckankar®, "Religion of the light and sound of God." The group claims 26,000 members. Followers believe in past lives, dream interpretation, and soul travel. Temple tours and free angel workshops are available.

Located at 7450 Powers Boulevard (Highway 17), Chanhassen, in Carver County; (800) LOVE-GOD; www.eckankar.org

SOUTHEASTERN

Including the counties of Blue Earth, Chisago, Dakota (southern portion), Dodge, Faribault, Fillmore, Freeborn, Goodhue, Houston, Isanti, Le Sueur, Mower, Nicollet, Olmsted, Rice, Scott (southern portion), Steele, Wabasha, Waseca, Winona, and Washington (eastern portion)

CHAPTER 2
SOUTHEASTERN MINNESOTA

Let us have harmony here!
—anonymous response to the bickering
at the founding of Harmony, Minnesota
(according to local legend)

Southeastern Minnesota, the state's Driftless Region, escaped the effects of the glacier that dominated other parts of the upper Midwest 10,000 years ago. It is a land full of giant bluffs, mysterious caverns, and sacred springs. Native American burial and effigy mounds are more plentiful in the southeast than in other parts of Minnesota, and the springs have always held great spiritual significance to Native Americans, who consider their waters to have healing powers.

The area is also full of ancient spirits and ghost towns, a result of small towns that projected big hopes on the future, only to be thwarted when the train stations that would ensure their economic success never materialized. Early pioneers who moved into the region after the 1851 treaty that opened the area for settlement once populated many of these towns.

One of those early pioneers was Episcopal Bishop Henry Benjamin Whipple, known as the "Apostle to the Indians," who served as a bridge between the Native Americans and the Christian church in the area. Bishop Whipple and the Native Americans treated each other with brotherly love that was very different from what was going on in other parts of the state and nation.

Southeastern Minnesota is also home to about 150 Amish families, the second largest settlement of Amish in the Midwest (the largest is just south of the border in Iowa). The area is also home to two of the largest stained-glass factories in the United States. The detailed glass products are shipped from Winona to churches and synagogues all over the nation.

Best of Southeastern Minnesota

- **CATHEDRAL OF THE MERCIFUL SAVIOR**, Faribault (oldest Episcopal cathedral in Midwest; stained glass depicts the story of the Dakota)
- **GAMMELKYRKAN**, Scandia (oldest church structure in Minnesota)
- **LENORA STONE UNITED METHODIST CHURCH**, Lenora (authentic pioneer church)
- **MINERAL SPRINGS PARK**, Owatonna (healing waters)
- **RED WING MOUNDS**, Red Wing (large effigy mounds)
- **RICE LAKE CHURCH**, Owatonna (historic church once at the edge of the wilderness)
- **SAINT MARY'S CHAPEL IN SAINT MARY'S HOSPITAL**, Mayo Foundation, Rochester (cathedral-like chapel at world-renowned hospital)
- **SAINT STANISLAUS CATHOLIC CHURCH**, Winona (intricate and stunning décor)
- **STONE CHURCH**, Cross of Christ Lutheran, Houston (beautiful church set at a rural crossroads)
- **VILLA MARIA**, Frontenac State Park (retreat center and convent set on bluffs overlooking the Mississippi)

NATIVE AMERICAN AND NATURAL SITES

Rocks and Bluffs

Taku-shkan-shkan ("Red Rock")

Many Native American tribes consider red rock boulders sacred. The Dakota called such boulders Taku-shkan-shkan, or "That which moves." The best-known red rock in the area sits in front of the Newport United Methodist Church in the town of Newport (although the rock was moved a number of times before it came to rest here). Newport, a few miles southeast of Saint Paul, was originally named Red Rock in honor of the stone. The Dakota designs painted on the rock have long since vanished.

According to John W. Armstrong, Ramsey County surveyor during the 1900s, "The boulder is but one of many granite boulders that were revered by the Dakota and other Native Americans in the Upper Midwest. Red was associated with blood, wounds, life, and shaman." Stephen R. Riggs, a missionary to the Dakota and author of the Dakota Grammar and Dictionary, wrote that the Dakota believed these boulders were solid forms of their gods. "They worship painting them red, decorating them with swan's down, and offering sacrifices. The boulder is 'toonkan,' or grandfather, by preeminence," wrote Riggs. "Every thing, even the . . . boulder, has a spirit."

Another red rock in the area is found between Kaposia and Mendota. Yet another was said to have been located on the south side of Red Rock Lake in

Eden Prairie, but it has since been lost.

Some other sacred medicine stones in Minnesota include those at Mille Lacs and the famous Three Maidens at Pipestone National Monument.

Red Rock is located in front of the Newport United Methodist Church, 1596 11th Avenue (at Glen Road), Newport, Washington County; (651) 459-2747. A historical marker stands nearby.

In-Yan-Teopa Rock

The In-Yan-Teopa Rock is a giant boulder perched high near the edge of a bluff, with markings etched into it that are sacred to the Dakota and Fox. There is a picnic area nearby with panoramic views of the Mississippi River.

Located at Frontenac State Park, near Frontenac, Goodhue County.

Chimney Rock

This 40-foot sandstone formation and Native American marker is best seen in the spring, fall, and winter due to plant growth in late summer. This site and others like it were used for vision quests and spiritual nurture by the Dakota and Ho-Chunk.

Located three miles south of Elba on Highway 74 at Whitewater State Park, Altura, Winona County; (507) 932-3007.

Faith, Hope, and Charity Bluffs

These three rocky bluffs are part of the 1,500-acre John Latsch State Park. Local steamboat captains named the bluffs for the Bible passage, "And now abideth faith, hope, charity, these three; but the greatest of these is charity." Indeed, Charity is the tallest of the three bluffs, which were a landmark to steamboat captains that they had arrived home. The area was the site of a steamboat landing and small logging town during the 1850s, but that facility and settlement have since disappeared. There is a spectacular view of the Mississippi River Valley from the peaks.

John Latsch State Park is located 12 miles northwest of Winona on Highway 61; (507) 932-3007.

Arrowhead Bluff

The Ho-Chunk and Dakota consider Arrowhead Bluff, located in a city park on the north side of Wabasha, sacred. The city was named for a Dakota chief's family, and Wabasha is the oldest city in Minnesota.

Located next to the Arrowhead Bluff Museum at the western edge of Wabasha on Highway 60. Wabasha is located on Highway 61, between Winona and Red Wing, in Wabasha County.

Interstate State Park

Look at a Wisconsin map with a little imagination and you'll see why part of the northwest corner of the state is known as Indianhead country—it's shaped like the head of a Native American chief. Amazingly, a natural rock formation created during the last glacier period in the bluffs at Interstate State Park bears the same likeness. The Ojibwe believed the face was the image of the god Winneboujou. Today, it's known as the Old Man of the Dalles (on the Wisconsin side of the river), and it's probably the most visited attraction in Interstate State Park, which has a sizeable counterpart across the river in Minnesota.

Other naturally formed figures in the area include the Devil's Chair, Devil's Kitchen, the Devil's Punch Bowl, the Devil's Footprint, and the Cross. Each formation was believed to have its own spirit.

The nation's first interstate park was founded on the Minnesota-Wisconsin border to protect the more than 100 unusual rock formations in the area, which include the Cauldron—60 feet deep and 20 feet wide. Also called the Bottomless Pit, it is the largest pothole on record. Pothole Trail is a short, self-guided mile hike through glacial potholes winding through the Dalles and into one of the giant holes.

The area has been inhabited for 6,000 years. It was here, in about 1770, that the Ojibwe battled the Dakota and Fox, enemies of both the Ojibwe and the white settlers. With the Ojibwe victory, white settlers were able to move into the area.

Located on Highway 8, Taylors Falls, Chisago County (Minnesota),
and Saint Croix Falls, Polk County (Wisconsin); (651) 465-5711.

Effigy and Burial Mounds

Red Wing Mounds

The area around Red Wing has the highest concentration of burial mounds in the state, the result of the Middle Mississippian people building large, flat-topped mounds and other sites near the confluence of the Mississippi and Cannon Rivers. There are two platform mounds: a flat-topped conical mound on Prairie Island northwest of town and a rectangular platform mound in a group of mounds between the Bryan and Silvernale sites. Bryan and Silvernale are the only mound sites in this area identified on the National Register of Historic Places. One flat-topped pyramidal mound measured 4 feet in height, 40 feet in width, and 60 feet in length when it was surveyed by Theodore H. Lewis in the mid-1880s.

Lewis, who first visited the region in 1849, wrote at that time of the Red Wing Mounds: "I remember that a row of mounds extended along the southwestern border of the Indian corn fields, the ground now occupied by streets and buildings in this city . . . scarcely any of them are now visible. . . . There were other mounds one half-mile southwest, on a flat or bench of land rising some 50 feet above the city [of Red Wing] ... the mounds [are] generally circular and even-shaped, and about 6 feet high in the center ... there was another mound on Barn Bluff." Demonstrations and exhibits of Dakota life are featured, and tours can be arranged by calling ahead.

The mounds are located near Heritage Village within the Prairie Island (Dakota) Indian Reservation, on the Cannon River northwest of Red Wing, Goodhue County; (651) 460-8050.

Great River Bluffs State Park

A mile-long, self-guided interpretive trail winding through Great River Bluffs State Park ends at a scenic overlook. Look for Native American effigy mounds and burial mounds along the route.

Located 20 miles southeast of Winona. From I-90, exit at County Highway 12 and follow the signs; (507) 643-6849.

Mounds Trail

Mounds Trail is a one-mile loop in the southeast corner of Frontenac State Park. The trail winds around 10 groups of mounds and two historic rock formations—one of which is shaped like a bridge and was the site of many Native American ceremonies and rites.

Maiden Rock, another site connected to Native American lore, is visible across the Mississippi River in Wisconsin. According to legend, a beautiful young Native American maiden had fallen in love, but not with the man she was expected to marry. Her family (her father in particular) and her tribe refused to listen to her pleadings to marry the man she loved, who was from another tribe. In some accounts, her beloved was sent away; in others, he was ordered to be killed. In one version of the story, the maiden jumped off the bluff in grief after watching her beloved die of an arrow wound.

Frontenac State Park is located on Highway 61 (10 miles southeast of Red Wing), near Frontenac, in Goodhue County; (651) 345-4582.

Afton Indian Mound

The late B. P. Squires accidentally uncovered this burial mound while plowing land between the Afton city garage and Holberg's Confectionary. The mound is now protected.

Located on the west side of the railroad tracks in the village of Afton (east of Saint Paul on the Saint Croix River), Washington County.

Springs and Caves

Mineral Springs Park

This park features a spring-fed waterfall. According to legend, the frail Princess Owatonna (literally, "Morally Straight" or "Honest") was restored to health by drinking the curative waters here, and tribes from around the region came to use the minnewaucan "curing water" bubbling up from the ground. Early pioneers also praised the pure spring water.

Located just south of Owatonna in Steele County, where Maple Creek crosses Highway 14/218 (near the junction with I-35).

Big Spring

Canfield Creek emerges from an underground cave to form a large spring in Forestville/Mystery Cave State Park, part of the Richard J. Doerr Memorial Hardwood Forest. Access is by hiking and a horseback-riding trail in the park. Native Americans, including Dakota and Ho-Chunk, considered such large springs to be particularly sacred and healing. Maps are available at the park office.

Located at the southern end of Forestville/Mystery Cave State Park, about 10 miles southeast of Preston on County Highway 12; (507) 352-5111.

Mystery Cave

In 1937, a farmer discovered this cavern, which turned out to be at least 12 miles long, filled with chambers and waterfalls. Mystery Cave is the largest cave system in the Upper Midwest and features a crystal-clear turquoise lake. Caves have historically been spiritual refuges, serving as ceremonial locations for many Native American tribes. The south branch of the Root River flows into Mystery Cave. The Root River flowage reappears at Seven Springs. Seven is a sacred number to many Native American tribes. You can sign up for guided tours and obtain maps at the park office.

Located at the far western end of Forestville/Mystery Cave State Park, about 10 miles southeast of Preston, Fillmore County; (507) 352-5111.

Niagara Cave

In 1924, a farmer, who kept losing his pigs in an open field, discovered Niagara Cave, considered one of the finest limestone caverns in the Midwest. Some of the ceilings in this cave are over 100 feet high, and there is a 60-foot waterfall. The site is considered sacred to the hundreds of couples who have been married by candlelight in its "crystal wedding chapel." Call about guided tours.

Located on Niagara Cave Road, about five miles southwest of Harmony, Fillmore County; (800) 837-6606 or (507) 886-6606; www.niagaracave.com; niagara@means.net

CATHOLIC SITES

Fort Beauharnois Chapel Site

In the 18th century, members of the Evangelical Missionary Society of Lausanne, Switzerland, were the first Europeans to settle the area along the Mississippi River bluffs near Frontenac. Father Louis Hennepin visited here in 1680, but it wasn't until 1727 that Fort Beauharnois was established. The chapel at the fort, originally established as a missionary outpost at Barn Bluff, was dedicated to Saint Michael, and the fort was named for Charles de la Baoishe, the Marquis de Beauharnois, then governor of New France. The fort was abandoned in 1736. A plaque commemorates the former chapel, considered to be the first Christian chapel in Minnesota.

Frontenac State Park is located on County Highway 2, one mile north of Highway 61, in Frontenac (10 miles southeast of Red Wing); (651) 345-3401.

Villa Maria Retreat Center

Villa Maria ("Mary's House") is a massive French chateau, erected in 1891, which was once a highly regarded convent school for girls. Today it is a retreat center, still operated by the Ursuline Sisters who came to "New France" (the area was part of Louisiana) in 1727.

Founded on the concept of a praying community living in unity, Villa Maria Retreat Center provides a secure interfaith setting for spiritual development. The retreat and conference center overlooks the Mississippi River and the bluffs of Wisconsin. The nonprofit center is sponsored by the Ursuline sisters and staffed by a ministry community of sisters and lay personnel.

Saint Angela Merici founded the Ursuline Sisters in 1535 in Italy, with missions of education, hospitality, liberation, and work for peace and justice. The order rapidly spread throughout Europe, and, later, to the United States. Today, the Ursulines serve in 33 countries and 14 states. In 1877, they arrived in Lake City, Minnesota, and three years later established a girls' school, Our Lady of the Lake. Less than five years later the enrollment had grown so much that a new, larger building was needed. General Israel Garrand gifted a large tract of land to the sisters in 1885 for the new school building, which was renamed Villa Maria Academy. Archbishop John Ireland dedicated the school and the new chapel there.

For 78 years, the academy drew students from all over the world. In 1969, a lightning strike started a fire, and the building was destroyed. It was later reopened with cooperation from Lutheran Pastor Ham Muss, and Villa Maria became an ecumenical retreat center. The center is described as "a haven of peace, prayerfulness and sacred space . . . (an interfaith retreat) for the purpose of assisting people in their spiritual and personal search for God." The center offers a labyrinth, retreat programs, spiritual direction, and meeting rooms. Villa Maria also offers an icon shop. Orthodox Christians consider icons "windows into heaven." Villa Maria is a designated importation center of icons from Meteora, Greece.

Located at 29847 County Highway 2, Frontenac; (651) 345-4582 or
(866) 244-4582; www.villamariaretreats.org; info@villamariaretreats.org.

Assisi Heights

In 1877, 25 Franciscan sisters (including two who were sisters by blood) established a community of Franciscan nuns in Rochester. There, the Sisters of the Third Order Regular of Saint Francis of the Congregation of Our Lady of Lourdes established Assisi Heights, a home on the highest hill in Olmsted County, which can be seen for miles. The Italian Romanesque architecture is similar to that of the Basilica of Saint Francis in Assisi, Italy. It features a tall bell tower with bells from Holland, beautiful stained-glass windows and mosaics, and marble from all over the world.

The Assisi Community Center in the facility is one of the largest conference/retreat centers in Minnesota, serving more than 40,000 people annually. The nonprofit center offers a variety of programs and individual retreats. Also ecumenical, it houses offices of the Evangelical Lutheran Church in America and the Rochester Montessori School.

Assisi Heights also features a labyrinth, a peace garden, and a monastery. The center offers tours three times a week and at other times by arrangement. Call ahead before visiting, as the monastery is very cautious about visitors. Guests are asked to sign in at the front desk and refrain from taking photographs.

Located at 1001 14th Street NW, Rochester; (507) 280-2180;
www.rochesterfranciscan.org/Assisi_Community_Center.htm.

Assisi Heights, Rochester

Other sites in southwestern Minnesota connected to the Sisters of Saint Francis, who operate Assisi Heights, include the Tau Center, Holy Spirit Retreat Center, and Saint Marys Hospital–Mayo Clinic.

TAU CENTER

This Franciscan retreat center is affiliated with Assisi Heights in Rochester. It accommodates over 60 people for overnight stays and over 150 for daytime programming.

Located at 511 Hilbert Street, Winona; (507) 454-2993.

HOLY SPIRIT RETREAT CENTER

People of all faiths are welcome to "listen and respond to the Spirit of God speaking within" at Holy Spirit Retreat Center. This retreat spans 30 acres of woods on Lake Elysian, about 15 miles east of Mankato. It features an outdoor grass labyrinth and the La Foresta Hermitage.

Located at 3864 420th Avenue, Janesville, Waseca County;
(507) 234-5712; www.rochesterfranciscan.org/Holy_Spirit.htm;
retreat@frontiernet.net
From Highway 14, take County Highway 3 (East Lake Elysian Road)
3.5 miles to the center.

SAINT MARYS HOSPITAL—MAYO CLINIC

After English-born physician William W. Mayo moved to Rochester in 1863 to examine inductees into the Union Army, he remained in the area and established a private practice. Twenty years later, a tornado destroyed much of Rochester, and Dr. Mayo and the Sisters of Saint Francis cared for the injured. They then built the first hospital in southern Minnesota. It was the beginning of what became the largest medical complex in the world, the Mayo Clinic, which is now made up of Saint Marys Hospital and the nearby Rochester Methodist Hospital. Today, about 1,300 patients arrive at the complex each day, and 250,000 are treated annually. Saint Marys Hospital is comprised of six buildings, one named for its founder and the other five for its administrators, all of them Franciscan sisters.

While the hospital ministers to the physical needs of its patients, it also provides ample opportunities for spiritual rehabilitation and renewal. Saint Marys Chapel is located on the first floor of the Domitilla Building. The Saint Francis Chapel is located on the fifth floor of the Francis Building, in the Tower section. All chapels are open 24 hours. Visitors are invited to write daily prayer requests in a book located in the chapels, so others may also pray for their intentions. Spiritual support booklets, called Care Notes, are also available in all chapels.

Doors of St. Marys Hospital-Mayo Clinic, Rochester

In addition, there are reflective spaces throughout the complex. The Groves Foundation Meditation Room, in the Mary Brigh Building (seventh floor) is also available 24 hours for persons of all faiths. This area, which faces east, is designed for quiet time and meditation. The Saint Francis Peace Garden, on the west side of the Generose Building, is open from dawn to dusk during the spring, summer, and fall. People of all faiths are welcome to use the garden for meditation and reflection. In addition, the hospital offers a diverse array of multifaith pastoral services.

Founded as a work of mercy, Saint Marys has a spirit that is best expressed in the motto Et sanavit omnos ("And He healed all"). And a Knights of Columbus plaque states its mission: "Through care of the sick, education of the medical and nursing professions, promotion of medical progress and research, Saint Marys gives service to God through service to man."

Tours of the grounds and buildings are available.

Located at 1216 Second Street SW, Rochester; (507) 255-5123.

Franciscan Retreat House

Franciscan Retreat is a facility owned and operated by the Conventual Franciscan Friars of Our Lady of Consolation Province. No one is turned away, regardless of ability to pay. "Everyone finds welcome, encouragement, direction, and community here," say the Franciscans. "There are no strangers."

The first thing the visitor sees upon entering the retreat house's chapel is the life-sized crucifix above the massive stone altar. The Christ is suspended, floating above the ground. The crucifix celebrates God's words to Saint Paul, "My grace is sufficient for you, for power is made perfect in weakness." Skylights and a dozen ground-level windows admit ever-changing light into the chapel, which is octagonal and seats 60.

The friars gather in prayer twice a day to celebrate mass and the Liturgy of the Hours. They include the requests of thousands of people. Anyone with special needs for prayer may contact the friars by phone, mail, or e-mail.

Located 16385 Saint Francis Lane, Prior Lake, Scott County;
(952) 447-2182; www.franciscanretreats.net; Director@FranciscanRetreats.net

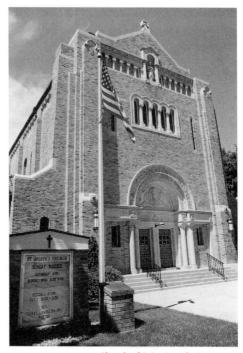

Church of Saint Joseph, Owatonna

Church of Saint Joseph

Formally established in 1891, this congregation's roots date back to 1854. The current building was built in 1922. Eighteen windows depicting the history of Christianity through the centuries are of British antique glass made with hand-blown pipes. A great arch opening into the sanctuary bears the Latin inscription, Esto Fidelis Usque Ad Mortem Et Tibi Dabo Coronam Vitae ("Be Thou Faithful Unto Me and I Will Give You the Crown of Life") in gold leaf.

The ceiling dome features a 2,000-square foot mural of the Trinity, in Romanesque coloring, with Mary and the saints on either side. The building is huge and imposing, and the church and rectory are joined by an enclosed walkway. A carving of the Holy Family is at the front entrance of the church. Showing Joseph as a protector of the infant Jesus and Mary, and it is believed to be the first such depiction in Catholic art.

Located at 512 South Elm Avenue (at the corner of East School Street), Owatonna, Steele County; (507) 451-4845; www.hickorytech.net/~stjoseph

Church of the Immaculate Conception

The original Church of the Immaculate Conception, which measured 20 by 30 feet, was built in Wabasha County in 1866, and the village of Conception was named for the church. It served the Irish and Germans immigrants, as well as settlers from New England, who had moved to the area during the 1850s. Just a few years after being built, the tiny church was replaced by a new structure, which is still standing today. The beautiful little white church with green blinds and a belfry is no longer in use as a parish. A pioneer cemetery is behind the church, "which has received the remains of many worthy pioneers of Highland township, some of whose graves are marked by pretentious monuments," according to a local newspaper.

Located on County Highway 18, in the tiny community of Conception (10 miles south of Wabasha), Wabasha County. For more information, call Holy Trinity/Saint Mary's Catholic Church in Oakridge at (507) 689-2351.

Saint Nicholas Church

This church, with a traditional 19th-century German Catholic interior, was built in 1868; it is no longer in regular use. The cemetery has German iron crosses and a beautiful gray crucifix of fossil stone.

Located near Freeburg on County Highway 249 at Crooked Creek, about eight miles east of Caledonia, in Houston County.

Saint Nicholas Catholic Church, near Caledonia

Saints Peter and Paul Parish

Erected in 1874, this church is one of the oldest in continuous use in southern Minnesota. The Jesuits renovated it in 1991. The church features stained glass from Germany and Austria, oak pews, and altars carved from oak, pine, and walnut. A local craftsman, Joseph Masberg, carved the statues of Saints Peter and Paul on the front steps.

Located at 105 North Fifth Street (at Mulberry Street), Mankato;
(507) 388-2995; www.sspeterandpaul.com

Our Lady of Good Counsel Chapel

The School Sisters of Notre Dame first came to Mankato in 1865, and in 1924, they erected a chapel at the site of their motherhouse in honor of Our Lady of Good Counsel. The Romanesque chapel overlooks the city and features a towering steeple and cross, as well as stained-glass windows crafted in Munich, Germany. Altars are of Italian marble, and the floor is of German ceramic. Oil paintings of the Stations of the Cross are from Munich. The site also features the Center for Spiritual Development.

Located at 170 Good Counsel Drive, Mankato; (507) 389-4200.

Saint Stanislaus Catholic Church

Saint Stanislaus Catholic Church is a monument to the Polish immigrants who came to Winona in the 1860s. One of the most intricately designed churches in the Midwest, the octagonal building is made of red brick with a neoclassical dome. The sanctuary seats 1,800. The lavish décor includes stone carvings and metal grille work.

Located at 601 East Fourth Street (at Carimona Street), Winona;
(507) 457-9662.

Saint Wenceslaus of Moravia Catholic Church (the Saco Church)

This church was originally named in honor of Saint Wenceslaus, an early Catholic king of Bohemia. It was later named after the nearby community of Saco. The building has been moved into the Village of Yesteryear, which is operated by the Steele County Historical Society. Built in 1891, the church still has its original furnishings, and a pump organ is still used for weddings. The church is open May through December; call for hours and tour information.

Located at 1448 Austin Road (along 18th Street SE), on the Steele County Fairgrounds, Owatonna; (507) 451-1420.

Saint Wenceslaus Catholic Church

Built in 1906, this is one of Minnesota's largest churches. The congregation, originally made up of newly arrived Czechs, dates back to 1856. The first log church was built in 1857 and burned down in 1863. The settlers considered moving back to eastern Europe, but Father Peter Maly talked them into staying. In 1868, a second church was completed. When it grew too large for the parish, the congregation erected the present building in 1907. The interior features several historic murals.

Located at 215 East Main Street, New Prague; (952) 758-3225;
www.saintwenceslaus.org

The Church of the Most Holy Trinity

This is another Czech Catholic Church in the southeastern part of the state. *Located at 4938 North Washington Street, Veseli (about 18 miles northwest of Faribault), Rice County.*

Cathedral of the Sacred Heart

In 1856, Bishop Cretin, the first bishop of Minnesota and the Dakotas, journeyed to Winona to celebrate the first recorded mass in the city. He also helped organize Winona's first Catholic parish. In 1857, Reverend Thomas Murray was appointed to the newly formed mission church, dedicated to Saint Thomas the Apostle. The Reverend Michael Pendergast became Winona's first resident priest in 1858. The congregation completed a new church three years later, and it served as the Pro-Cathedral for the Diocese of Winona until the dedication of the Cathedral of the Sacred Heart in 1952. The cathedral was renovated in 1982; among the new features is a Gress-Miles pipe organ.

Located at 360 Main Street, Winona; (507) 452-4770; www.hbci.com/~cathedra

Church of the Holy Trinity

In the mid-1800s, many area Catholic settlers attended church in Elba, a Luxembourger-German settlement about 20 miles west of Winona. In 1869, a stone church was erected in Rollingstone, a town midway between Elba and Winona. The new building, which still stands today, was dedicated in July 1869 by Bishop Grace of Saint Paul and named Holy Trinity. The sanctuary has been redesigned and the entire church redecorated.

Located at 83–91 Main Street, Rollingstone; (507) 689-2351 or (507) 689-2251.

EPISCOPAL SITES

Cathedral of Our Merciful Savior

This cathedral, the first established by the American Episcopal Church in Minnesota, was completed in 1869 under the state's first Episcopal bishop, Henry Benjamin Whipple. Known as the "Apostle to the Indians," he was a great advocate of Native American rights and is known for his mission work with the Dakota and Ojibwe. Bishop Whipple interceded with President Lincoln on behalf of 303 Dakota that the U.S. government had accused of murder in the Dakota Conflict of 1862. As a result, 265 Dakota lives were spared. The church features a stained-glass window depicting a pipe and a broken war club, a gift from the Dakota in thanks for Bishop Whipple's help.

In the cathedral hangs an icon of Enmegahbowh (see "Saint Columba Mission" in chapter 4), the first Native American ordained in the Episcopal Church. This imposing Gothic cathedral is made of stone, wood, and glass. The church and the nearby guild house are both on the National Register of Historic Places. Call ahead to check visiting hours.

Located at 515 Second Avenue NW, Faribault; (507) 334-7732.

Chapel of the Good Shepherd

Bishop Henry Whipple, who also established the Cathedral of Our Merciful Savior, founded the Shattuck School for Boys and its Chapel of the Good Shepherd in 1865. The facility is now a co-ed school and is open for drive-through visits of the campus. The chapel is on the National Register of Historic Places.

Located at 100 Shumway Avenue, Faribault; (800) 421-2724 or (507) 332-5618.

Stained Glass in Winona

Winona, population 30,000, is known as the "stained glass capital of the United States." The nation's two largest art-glass companies, along with another smaller studio, are located here, supplying stained glass for many churches. The second largest company, Conway Universal Studios, offers informal tours of its operation at 503 Center Street. Call (507) 452-9209 to arrange a tour. An informational brochure is available from the Winona Convention and Visitors Bureau.

Grace Memorial Episcopal Church

Manufactured in 1900, the chancel window of this church depicts the two Marys at the tomb on Easter morning. It was made by Tiffany Studios of New York at a cost of $3,000. The building is on the National Register of Historic Places.

Located at 205 East Third Street, Wabasha; (651) 565-4827.

Church of the Holy Comforter
(Brownsville Church)

Currently used only for weddings, this little church at the edge of a bluff was built in 1869 and renovated in 1980. At different times it was the Methodist Episcopal Church and the Emmanuel Evangelical Lutheran Church. It is on the National Register of Historic Places and is open by appointment.

Located at 104 History Lane (adjacent to the Houston County Fairgrounds), Caledonia. For more information, contact Shirley Johnson at (507) 725-3884 or (507) 896-2291.

All Saints Church

In 1856, a small group of Episcopal women, many recently resettled from upstate New York in the new town of Northfield, formed the Ladies Social Circle "for the benefit of the Episcopal church." Their group later evolved into the All Saints Church. The parish raised funds to build the rural Gothic church building, which was designed by Rector Solomon Burleson, using plans from Richard Upjohn's book *Rural Architecture.* The building was dedicated in 1867, and the steeple was added in 1879. It is on the National Register of Historic Places.

Located at 419 Washington Street, Northfield; (507) 645-7417;
www.allsaintsnorthfield.org

Church of the Transfiguration

The area near the Minnesota River southwest of the Twin Cities was settled primarily by Irish and German immigrants, who brought with them their own worship practices. The church's unique Prairie Gothic structure has wooden buttresses. Erected in 1868 on land donated by Judge Andrew G. Chattfield, the church had served the community dating back to 1854, with the arrival of the missionary Father Timothy Wilcox of Saint Paul.

In its early years, the church thrived, but its membership dwindled through the years until there were only about a dozen members in the 1950s. The church was officially closed and the building deteriorated. The Scott County Historical Society has worked to save the structure, which is on the National Register of Historic Places.

Located at Walnut and Church Streets, Belle Plaine, Scott County; (952) 445-0378; www.scottcountyhistory.org/sitesepiscopalchurch.html

Church of the Advent

Although its parishioner numbers have waxed and waned, the Church of the Advent has been a strong spiritual presence in the Farmington community since 1871. The structure is on the National Register of Historic Places.

Located at 412 Oak Street, Farmington, Dakota County; (651) 460-6636.

Saint Mary's Episcopal Church

The two wooden crosses at Saint Mary's altar were carved from black walnut trees from a local resident's farm. The church is on the shore of the Saint Croix River, south of Afton and north of Hastings.

Located at 8435 County Highway 21, Basswood Grove, Washington County; (651) 436-1872.

Christ Church

Reverend Edward Wells established Christ Church in 1858; the congregation erected the present church building in 1876. The Foot Memorial Chapel was added in 1903, and the steeple completed in 1912. The church, located in historic downtown Red Wing, features limestone from nearby Barn's Bluff, Gothic arched windows, and an impressive gable entry.

Located at 321 West Avenue, Red Wing, Goodhue County; (651) 388-0411.

LUTHERAN SITES

Faith Lutheran Church of Black Hammer

The tiny community of Black Hammer, west of Caledonia, got its name many years ago when Knut Olson Bergo woke up one morning and saw that a prairie fire had spread across the nearby hammer-shaped hill. It reminded him of a hill near his former home in Norway, called Sard (Black) Hammer.

After the fire, a unique rock formation atop the hill became visible. It had been built in the likeness of a woman and was quite old. It became known as "the Stone Lady." Stories of who built her abounded, and some believed that Native Americans, possibly the Dakota or Ho-Chunk, were responsible. Some people also believed that there was once a "Stone Man" and "Stone Child" next to the Stone Lady.

Immigrant Lutherans viewed the Stone Lady as mysterious and spiritually protective of the area, and in 1859, they erected a church in view of the hill where she resides. The Stone Lady as well as the original church structure still exist; the church building today stands behind a newer façade that serves as an entryway. Once inside, the visitor faces a set of stairs that lead to the original narthex, interior, and altar. The cemetery has graves dating back to the 1860s.

The church is located on Black Hammer Drive at County Highway 4, about five miles north of Spring Grove, Houston County; (507) 498-5154. The Stone Lady is on the opposite side of County Highway 4 from the church.

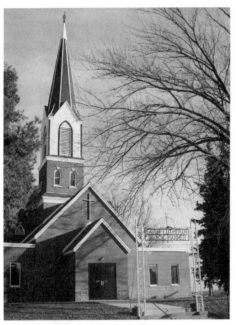

Faith Lutheran Church of Black Hammer,
near Spring Grove

Cross of Christ Lutheran Stone Church

The Stone Church, built by a congregation established in 1855, has one of the oldest cemeteries in the county still in use. The church building is made of cream-colored stones, in contrast to the surrounding wooded hills, and looks almost new despite its age. The Cross of Christ Lutheran Church maintains the property and cemetery. The church is used occasionally for services, including an ancestral reunion held annually for those with pioneer forebears interred in the cemetery.

*The Stone Church is located at 6985 Highway 76, Houston.
For more information, contact the Cross of Christ Lutheran Church at
(507) 896-3104 or (507) 896-3102.*

Vista Lutheran Church

This red brick and stone church, built in 1908, is a historically significant structure that embodies the Swedish heritage of Waseca County. It features several elements of the Gothic Revival style of architecture. Beautiful stenciling decorates the walls and ceiling, and the carved pulpit is positioned high above the congregation. The church sits at the crossroads of two country roads, affording a magnificent view of the farmland and fields of Waseca County. The structure is on the National Register of Historic Places.

*Located on County Highway 20, about 10 miles south of Waseca,
Waseca County. For information, contact the Waseca County Historical Society,
(507) 835-7700; www.historical.waseca.mn.us/vista.htm*

Vasa Lutheran Church

Here, in one of the most thoroughly Swedish communities in America, this church was built in 1869 and named after the Swedish King Gustav Vasa. The red-brick Greek Revival structure is an imposing sight. Soon after it was built, the church became home to Pastor Eric Norelius, who founded Gustavus Adolphus College, and it was also the site of the state's first orphanage. Located near the church is the Vasa Museum, dedicated to the town, one of Minnesota's first Swedish-American settlements. Considered a center for early Swedish culture, the church has been restored to its 1901 appearance.

The church is located at 15235 Norelius Road, Vasa, Goodhue County; (651) 258-4327. The little town is midway between Cannon Falls and Red Wing off Highway 19.

Hauge Lutheran Church

A Norwegian congregation founded this church in 1859, and the first building ("The Old Stone Church") was erected in 1888. The present building was built in 1902.

Located at 317 Third Avenue, Kenyon, Goodhue County; (507) 789-6343. Kenyon is about 15 miles east of Faribault, off Highway 60.

Christdala Evangelical Swedish Lutheran Church

The first Swedish immigrants to Rice County built Christdala Evangelical Swedish Lutheran Church in 1878 in a late Gothic Revival style. Its original Swedish name was Den Svenska Evangeliska Lutherska Christdala Forsamlingen. This is the original building—it has never been moved or altered. Also, its nearby one-acre cemetery and the surrounding property overlooking Circle Lake appear pretty much the same as they did when the early Swedish immigrants arrived here.

Between 1840 and 1930, more than 1,300,000 Swedish immigrants settled in the United States, primarily in Minnesota. The first 40 years of this church's existence correspond with the high point of the Swedish emigration to the area. The congregation reached a peak membership in 1890, but by 1918 it had declined to fewer than 100 members. With only thirty members of the congregation in the 1950s, services were terminated in the 1960s and the congregation disbanded in 1966.

The Christadala Cemetery Association maintains the grounds, building, and cemetery. The church is listed on the National Register of Historic Places.

Located on County Highway 1, two miles west of the community of Millersburg on the north edge of Circle Lake, Rice County. The church is about 15 miles north of Faribault.

The Swedish Circle Tour

The area just north of the Twin Cities has several other noteworthy, historic Lutheran churches. With the exception of Saint John's Lutheran, the following are part of the Swedish Circle in Minnesota, a self-guided tour of historic Lutheran churches in Chisago and Isanti Counties. To find out more about the tour, call (651) 257-4773.

• ZION EVANGELICAL LUTHERAN CHURCH. Organized in 1874. At 28005 Old Towne Road, one mile south of Highway 8 and Old Towne Road, Chisago City; (651) 257-2713.

• FIRST EVANGELICAL (SWEDISH) LUTHERAN CHURCH. Organized in 1860. The current building was built in 1903 and contains a history room. At 651 Chestnut Street, Taylors Falls, Chisago County; (651) 465-5265.

• IMMANUEL LUTHERAN CHURCH. Organized in 1887. A historic cemetery is adjacent. The church is northwest of Taylors Falls along Highway 8 in Almelund, Chisago County; (651) 583-2340.

• FISH LAKE LUTHERAN CHURCH. Organized in 1867. The interior features a Swedish painted ceiling and walls, an original 1905 mural, and a Hultgren and Lane Tracker Organ. Tours are available by calling (651) 674-4252. Located seven miles northwest of North Branch on County Highway 10, Chisago County.

• SVENSKA MISSION KYRKA I SODRE MAPLE RIDGE (Swedish Mission Church of South Maple Ridge). On the National Register of Historic Places, but currently vacant. On County Highway 1 in Braham, Isanti County.

• SAINT JOHN'S LUTHERAN CHURCH. Established in 1870 as a German Evangelical Church, Saint John's is now a Missouri Synod Lutheran church. The structure is on the National Register of Historic Places. On County Highway 5, near the village of Bradford, Isanti County.

Chisago Lake Lutheran Church, Center City

Chisago Lake Lutheran Church

The second oldest Lutheran church in Minnesota, this congregation was organized in May 1854. The current structure, built in Center City on an isthmus in 1889, sits on the site of the original church, built in 1856. The church features a historic tapestry, a monument to the founder of the synod, and a pioneer cemetery. Center City's historic district is nearby, which recalls the days of the first permanent Swedish settlement in Minnesota. Call for guided tours.

Located on County Road 9 in Center City, Chisago County;
(651) 257-6300.

Gammelkyrkan and the Elim Lutheran Church

Built in 1856, Gammelkyrkan is the oldest church structure in Minnesota, having been moved several times from its original location at nearby Hay Lake. Another related structure, the parsonage (the oldest in the state), was built in 1868. Both are part of the Swedish Immigrant History Museum, an 11-acre site with four other original buildings erected by the area's first Swedish settlers. Upon seeing the church, traveler and author Fredrika Bremer is said to have exclaimed, "Hvilket herrligt Nytt Skandinavien kunde ej Minnesota bli!"

63

("What a glorious new Scandinavia might not Minnesota become!") The new Elim Lutheran Church building is across the street from the museum.

Located at 20880 Olinda Trail (off Highway 97), Scandia, Washington County; (651) 433-5053.

Saint Olaf College

Founded in 1874 by Norwegian immigrants, the "pretty college on the hill" is on Northfield's west side. At one time the college was so conscious of its heritage that any student more than one-fourth Norwegian had to study the Norwegian language.

The King's Room Corridor includes the Steensland Gallery, which is open to the public. Visitors can walk a three-mile nature trail that begins by the Skoglund Center. The Boe Chapel is the heart of the campus, with its beautiful stained-glass windows, including one depicting the college's patron saint. It also houses a large organ used for worship services and by the music department. The chapel is on the National Register of Historic Places.

The Saint Olaf Choir is known around the world; the choir represented the United States at the 1988 Olympics in Seoul, Korea.

Located on Saint Olaf Avenue off Highway 19, Northfield. For more college information, call (507) 646-2222; gallery information, (507) 646-3556; events information, (507) 646-3040; www.stolaf.edu

Mount Olivet Retreat Center

"Rooted in Christ, the Mount Olivet Retreat Center is dedicated to nurturing the spiritual, emotional and intellectual growth of all people through caring and creative ministries, quiet reflection and a reverence for life." The retreat occupies 150 acres of secluded and rolling prairie and woodlands. Daytime and overnight retreats are available for individuals and groups. The center is ecumenical and handicap accessible.

Located at 7984 257th Street West, Farmington, Dakota County; (952) 469-2175.

Camp Omega

Opened in 1964, Camp Omega is a retreat facility and summer camp near Waterville. Visitors can camp, canoe, sail, and ride pontoon boats on 417-acre Horseshoe Lake. According to the camp's materials, "The most important part of Camp Omega is our Christ centered ministry! We are here to help lead your next group gathering (in any capacity that you need), or you can attend some of our sponsored retreats. Camp Omega has 76 acres with over 7,000 feet of shoreline." The camp is affiliated with the Lutheran Church (Missouri Synod).

Located at 22750 Lind Avenue (about four miles northeast of Waterville), Le Sueur County; (507) 685-4401; www.campomega.org; info@campomega.org

ᎷETHODIST ᏚITES

Rice Lake Church

All that remains of the pioneer village that once stood at this site, seven miles east of Owatonna, is a little white church built by Methodist settlers in 1857. Although no longer in use, the church is in good condition, and the grounds are nicely maintained. The town thrived until 1865 when the railroad chose a route that bypassed the community. Over the years, the church has been used by several denominations. Visitors can enjoy a marvelous view of Rice Lake and the state park named after it, just to the south.

Located on County Highway 19 at County Highway 20. For more information, contact Rice Lake State Park, RR 3, Box 45, Owatonna, MN 55060; (507) 451-7406.

Rice Lake Church, near Owatonna

Ottawa Methodist Church

"The Little Stone Church in the Valley" is the oldest Methodist church in the state, built in 1858 with native limestone. Completely restored, it features period fixtures and is maintained by the Ottawa Chapter of the Le Sueur County Historical Society. An annual church service is held the Sunday after Labor Day.

Located one-half mile south of Le Sueur on Highway 112; (507) 665-2861; www.lchs.mus.mn.us/county/ottawa.html

Lenora Stone United Methodist Church

Primarily a history lesson today, the restored Lenora Stone Church is the oldest church in Fillmore County, built in 1865. Because the railroad that was planned to go through Lenora never materialized, the town and church eventually dwindled in size and the church closed in the 1920s. The church is now open to the public for special events, including holiday services conducted beneath the light of oil lamps, with the pastor and others clothed in period costumes. Visitors experience an atmosphere of what it was like to be a 19th-century pioneer.

Located at the intersection of County Highways 23 and 24, Lenora (seven miles east of Harmony), Fillmore County; (507) 545-2641.

Lenora Stone United Methodist Church, near Harmony

Portland Prairie Methodist Episcopal Church

This building was built in 1877 after congregants, settlers from Rhode Island and Massachusetts, had spent many years meeting in local homes. They built a school the same year. For many years, the church was served by circuit riders (pastors) who ministered to several rural congregations and traveled between them. Regular services were held until 1935, and special services are still held each year. The church is associated with the Caledonia United Methodist Church, and the cemetery there is still in use. The original church building is on the National Register of Historic Places.

Located off Highway 76, near Houston (about 17 miles west of La Crescent), Houston County.

Newport United Methodist Church Log Cabin

In 1840, the Reverend Benjamin T. Kavanaugh of Ohio built a two-story log structure at Red Rock (now the city of Newport). The building housed the earliest known Methodist chapel in the state, along with a meeting room and school.

The mission disbanded in 1843, and the congregation eventually moved to its present location, where the log cabin meeting area and school have been preserved. The Newport United Methodist Church building is at the same location.

Located at 1596 11th Avenue (at Glen Road), Newport, Washington County; (651) 459-2747.

Taylors Falls United Methodist Church, Taylor Falls

Taylors Falls United Methodist Church

This is the second oldest Methodist church building in continuous use in Minnesota. In 1861, two years after the establishment of the congregation, the parishioners built the white pine, Greek Revival building, reminiscent of New England churches, for $2,500 on donated land. The church served as the hub of early Methodist circuit riders from the 1850s. The congregation completed a restoration for its 125th anniversary in 1984. The building is part of the Taylors Falls Angel Hill Historic District.

Located at 290 West Government Street, Taylors Falls, Chisago County; (651) 465-6635.

PRESBYTERIAN AND CONGREGATIONAL SITES

Congregational Church of Faribault

In 1856, a congregation of the Congregational Church of Faribault built its first church. They constructed the present building, with a 114-foot wooden bell tower, 10 years later, utilizing limestone from a quarry site east of the city. The stained-glass window behind the altar, depicting the Resurrection, was constructed at Tiffany Studios in New York. The Mary Leavens Chapel, named for a beloved Sunday school teacher, was added to the building in 1910. Today the church features a labyrinth and is on the National Register of Historic Places.

Located at 222 Third Avenue NE, Faribault; (507) 334-5910; www.congregationalucc.org; uccfbo@means.net

Peace United Church of Christ

Formerly the Evangelical Church of Peace, this church was organized in 1879, and reorganized in 1885 as German Evangelical Friendens Church. It became the Peace UCC Crooked Creek in 1960. The church is surrounded by rolling hills and has a historic graveyard.

Located at 3272 County Highway 249, west of Freeburg, Houston County.

Peace United Church of Christ, Freeburg

Skinner Memorial Chapel, Carleton College

Carleton College was founded as Northfield College by the Minnesota Conference of Congregational Churches in 1866. The name was changed in

1871 to honor an early benefactor, William Carleton, of Charlestown, Massachusetts, who had bestowed a gift of $50,000—the single largest contribution ever made to a western college up to that time. He did not even request the name change. Today the chapel holds Taize Vespers (an ecumenical Christian style of common prayer based on singing) and weekly services representing a variety of faiths. The chapel is on the National Register of Historic Places.

Located on First Street between Winona and College Avenues, Northfield, Rice County.

Saint Paul's United Church of Christ

Organized in 1868 as Saint Paul's Evangelical Church by eight German families, this church has belonged to the German Lutheran Synod, the Evangelical Synod of North America, and the German Reformed Church. In 1957 the Evangelical and Reformed Church united with the Congregational Christian Church to form the United Church of Christ. This traditional white church building, with an interior that has not changed significantly over the years, sits just beside the road on a hill. Its cemetery is well over 100 years old.

Located at 12925 County Highway 9, Eyota (about 15 miles east of Rochester), Olmsted County; (507) 545-2495.

Interior Saint Paul's United Church of Christ, Eyota

First Presbyterian Church

In 1876, lighting hit the roof of this church, causing a fire, but its walls survived because they were wet from the accompanying rainstorm. Reconstruction was completed in 1909. The structure is on the National Register of Historic Places.

Located at 602 Vermillion Street, Hastings, Dakota County; (651) 437-6527; www.fpresby.org

First Presbyterian Church of Stillwater

The first Presbyterian congregation in the area formed in 1849, making this church one of the first Protestant churches in the Northwest Territory. The parishioners erected the current building in 1999.

Located at 6201 Osgood Avenue North, Stillwater, Washington County; (651) 439-4380; church@fpcstillwater.org

$\mathcal{O}$THER $\mathcal{C}$HRISTIAN $\mathcal{S}$ITES

Saint Matthew's Evangelical and Reformed Church

Behind the Cottage Grove United Church of Christ near the Old Cottage Grove cemetery is a quaint white clapboard church that was once Saint Matthew's Evangelical and Reformed Church. From 1874 until the 1950s, Saint Matthew's served the local German community. The building is recognized as a local historic place, but it is not presently in use.

First Baptist Church, Minnesota City

German immigrants formed the First Baptist congregation in 1852 and erected a church in 1875. That building still stands, making it the oldest Baptist church in Minnesota. In the mid-1960s, the congregation merged with the First Baptist Church of Winona. Occasional services are held. A women's group maintains the facility and grounds, and tours can be arranged through the First Baptist Church of Winona (see the following).

Located on Highway 61 in Minnesota City (about five miles north of Winona), Winona County.

First Baptist Church, Winona

Founded in 1855, this is the second oldest Baptist church in Minnesota. The current stone building was erected in 1888 and includes many historical displays as well as the original stained glass. Tours can be arranged.

Located at 368 West Broadway Street, Winona; (507) 452-9133.

The Morovian Church in Southeastern Minnesota

Berea Morovian Church, near St. Charles

The Moravian Church is one of the few Protestant groups that predate Martin Luther's 1517 revolt against the Catholic Church. Moravians and Bohemians, then known as the Hussites, were persecuted for many years. Today, the Moravians' guiding principle is "In essentials, unity, in non-essentials, liberty, and in all things, love."

The first Moravian church in Minnesota was **Bethany Moravian Church** (named for a village in biblical Palestine), founded in 1867. The town of Bethany, about 15 miles west of Winona, was platted in 1891 and named after the church. This was the beginning of a significant immigration of middle Europeans to the area. Later the congregation merged with Hebron Moravian Church to form Our Savior's Moravian Church, and the Bethany Moravian Church building was destroyed in 1979.

There are many historic Moravian churches nearby, including the **Berea Moravian Church**, eight miles northeast of Saint Charles; **Our Savior's Church** in Altura; **Christ's Community Church** in Maple Grove; **Main Street Moravian Church** in Northfield; **Lake Auburn Church** in Victoria; and **Waconia Church** in Waconia. The **Zoar Moravian Church**, on the National Register of Historic Places, is in Chaska, a suburb near the Twin Cities (see the separate listing in chapter 1).

The Amish in Minnesota

Minnesota is home to the second largest Amish community in the Midwest. (The largest is spread over Buchanan, Fayette, and Clayton Counties in northeastern Iowa.) The Amish settlement in southern Minnesota, the only one in the state, is located around the towns of Canton, Lanesboro, Preston, and Harmony in Fillmore County.

The Amish trace their origins to 16th-century Switzerland, when a religious group called the Anabaptists ("rebaptizers") formed a fellowship. They

71

believed that people should be baptized as adults rather than as infants, and they wanted a church that was not under the control of the state. One of the Anabaptist groups developed into the Mennonites, named after a former Catholic priest, Menno Simons, who joined the group in 1536. When Jacob Amman later broke from the Mennonites over a disagreement about excommunication, he formed a separate group, the Amish. While the Mennonites had taught pacifism and separated themselves from society, the Amish went a step further, with the Old Order Amish retaining the dress and customs of the 18th century. Their wide-brimmed hats and horse-and-buggy teams are familiar sights in several parts of the Midwest.

Old Order Amish dress in plain clothes: the men in dark suits, the women in long dresses. They do not use modern electronic equipment or machinery; even buttons are forbidden. And, of course, the Amish use buggies rather than automobiles for transportation. When driving in Amish areas, one is asked to be respectful of the slow-moving vehicles. Also visitors should not take photographs of Amish people, as photography is considered a forbidden "graven image."

Today there are about 150 Amish families in southern Minnesota. They have several church "districts" and a number of one-room schools. Tours are offered on weekdays and Saturdays through several area agencies. The "Amish Buggy Byway" is another name for the stretch of Highway 52, between Highway 16 at Preston and Highway 44 at Prosper; black, horse-drawn buggies are frequently seen along the way.

Tours are available through Michel's Amish Tours, Fillmore, (507) 886-5392; Amish Country Tours, Harmony, (507) 886-2303; and R and M Amish Touring, Lanesboro, (507) 467-2128.

A road sign in Amish country

RETREAT CENTERS

ARC Ecumenical Retreat Center

This nonprofit ecumenical retreat center serves a variety of faith traditions. Its mission is to encourage people of God to integrate A (Action), R (Reflection), and C (Celebration) into their lives. Founded in 1977 by the Greeley Grandy Union Church as an interfaith chapel, the center has a sign reading "Joyful, Simple, Merciful" over the door.

The staff can facilitate or lead individual or group retreats at its 90-acre pine and hardwood forest. A hermitage, called Poustinia ("Desert Space"), is also available. Guests are welcome to walk around the Native American mounds nearby.

Located at 1680 373rd Avenue NE (just off Highway 65, eight miles north of Cambridge), Stanchfield, Isanti County; (763) 689-3540; arcretreat@hotmail.com

Hazelden Renewal Center

Founded in 1949, Hazelden is a well-known nonprofit foundation and a pioneering model of care for alcoholism and other addictions. An international provider of treatment, recovery, research, training, and education, Hazelden offers programs, services, and publications for individuals, families, and communities affected by chemical dependency and who are in 12-Step programs.

The Renewal Center, situated on a tranquil, 500-acre wooded campus, "is a place for nourishing the mind, heart, soul, and body of those traveling the path of recovery." It offers regular programs on spirituality and recovery and is designed to meet the spiritual needs of individuals who are actively involved in any 12-Step program, with a minimum of two months of sobriety required.

The lodge is an ongoing service of the Renewal Center. Intended for the enrichment of those working with 12-Step recovery, it has a minimum seven-day stay.

Limited scholarships are available.

Located at 15245 Pleasant Valley Road, Center City, Chisago County; (651) 213-4104 or (800) 262-4882; www.hazelden.org/renewalcenter

The Sanford Memorial Healing Garden

On the grounds of Trinity Hospital in Farmington, the healing garden is a place for patients, family members, and the public to retreat, clear their minds, and enjoy the plants and flowers. A brick-and-cement labyrinth has just been added, and a canvas labyrinth accommodates wheelchairs.

Located at 3410 213th Street West, Farmington, Dakota County; (651) 460-1169.

$\mathcal{O}$THER $\mathscr{S}$ITES

The Peace Fountain

Designed by local sculptor Charles Eugene Gagnon, this bronze sculpture and fountain is dedicated to world peace. Located in downtown Rochester, the fountain and its small outdoor plaza were created to foster serenity. The fountain is made of circular tiers of bronze doves representing the 50 states and the seven continents.

Located at Centerpiece Galleria in downtown Rochester.

First Unitarian Universalist Church

The first Universalist sermon in Minnesota was preached by the Reverend Isaac Westfall in Olmsted County in 1860. A congregation formed in 1866, and the fledgling group constructed a small building for $2,200. In 1877, a larger structure, named Grace Church, was erected, and journalist Horace Greeley attended a service there. In 1962, the church formally changed its name to First Unitarian Universalist Church to recognize the national merger of the Unitarian and Universalist denominations. The group's present building was erected in 1968. Workers saved stained-glass windows from the old church, and they are a highlight of the current building.

Located at 1727 Walden Lane SW, Rochester; (507) 282-5209; www.uurochmn.org; office@uurocjmn.org

Wat Lao Minnesota

Wherever there's a wat (temple), there's a Lao community dedicated to preserving and practicing Buddhist precepts, according to Wat Lao Minnesota. Traditionally, the majority of Lao-speaking people have been Theravada Buddhists. In recent years, Lao Buddhist wats have sprung up around the world to care for the spiritual needs of Lao immigrants. Buddhist temples welcome all seekers regardless of ethnic background. Wat Lao Minnesota is a nonprofit organization that belongs spiritually to the Lao Buddhist community and to all people who helped support the establishment of this religious institution.

Located at 22605 Cedar Avenue South, Farmington, Dakota County; (952) 469-1692; www.angelfire.com/mn2/watlao

*L*a Crescent

The town of La Crescent got its name as the result of the "holy war" it waged with the residents of La Crosse, Wisconsin, directly across the Mississippi River. In the 19th century, the two towns were bitter rivals. In reaction to the name La Crosse (the symbol of Christianity), the Minnesota townsfolk named their community La Crescent (the symbol of Islam). This was despite the fact that La Crosse was named for the sport of lacrosse.

Hokyo-Ji Monastery Retreat (Hokyoji)

The Hokyoji (interpreted as "Catching the Moon Temple") has a natural setting that is ideal for sesshins (gatherings) and family activities. The Minnesota Zen Center in Minneapolis owns and operates this retreat in southern Minnesota near the Iowa border, just one mile north of New Albin, Iowa, the largest town in the area. The beautiful and peaceful retreat is located on 280 acres amidst farmland close to the Mississippi, near the borders of Minnesota, Iowa, and Wisconsin. As yet there is no dormitory for visitors, but tents can be set up for overnight stays, and some practitioners sleep in the zendo (temple building) on the grounds.

Located in the southeastern corner of Minnesota, in Houston County, off Highway 26; (317) 251-0755. During meditation and sesshins, the phone may not be answered. For further information, contact the Minnesota Zen Center in Minneapolis; (612) 822-5313; mnzenctr@aol.com

B'nai Israel Synagogue

Rabbi David Freedman serves as a chaplain in the Mayo Foundation hospitals and clinic and as rabbi for this Reform congregation. The chaplaincy is a joint program of the Minneapolis Jewish Federation, Saint Paul United Jewish Fund and Council, B'nai B'rith, and the Mayo Foundation.

Located at 621 Second Street SW (near Saint Marys Hospital), Rochester; (507) 288-5825; www.bnaisrael.org; bisrebbe@aol.com or bnaisrael@aol.com

*I*SLAMIC *C*ENTERS

Dar Abi Bakr Islamic Center

This 1998 mosque is part of the Muslim Student Association at Minnesota State University, Mankato, 329 East Plum Street, Mankato; (507) 386-1797.

Islamic Center of Winona

Located at 54 East Third Street, Winona; (507) 453-9961.

Rochester Islamic Center

Located at 322 Broadway South, Rochester; (507) 282-8087.

SOUTHWESTERN

*Including the counties of Benton, Big Stone, Brown, Carver,
Chippewa, Cottonwood, Faribault, Jackson, Kandiyohi, Lac qui Parle,
Martin, McLeod, Meeker, Murray, Nicollet, Nobles, Pipestone, Pope,
Redwood, Renville, Rock, Sherburne, Sibley, Stearns, Stevens, Swift,
Watonwan, Wright, and Yellow Medicine*

CHAPTER 3
SOUTHWESTERN MINNESOTA

The peoples of this region share a legacy.
That legacy is a knowledge that
we are all immigrants.
—Scott Anfinson

Our spirituality comes from the heart and
is as diverse as we are individuals.
—Jim Cochrane, manager of Pipestone
Indian Shrine Association

Southwestern Minnesota is home to probably the most notable Native American historical site in North America—Pipestone National Monument, where, it is said, humankind was created. Native Americans all over North America use the unique red stone found there for sacred peace pipes. Jeffers Petroglyphs Historic Site contains 2,000 petroglyphs—the largest group of these mysterious carvings in the world. But there is also great spiritual variety in this part of the state. Protestant missionaries shaped the history of the area, especially Lutheran farmers who settled here after the expulsion of the Dakota following the 1862 uprising. Although many Catholic churches are in the area—especially in Stearns County—this part of Minnesota is still heavily Protestant.

ꝶest of Southwestern Minnesota

• **ASSUMPTION CHAPEL** ("the Grasshopper Chapel"), Cold Spring
(dedicated to miracles and built to inspire)
• **DANEBOD LUTHERAN CHURCH**, Tyler (unusual design on Danish
folk school property)
• **JEFFERS PETROGLYPHS**, Cottonwood County (accessible petroglyphs)
• **LAC QUI PARLE MISSION**, Montevideo (first Protestant mission in
the west)
• **MAMRE FREE LUTHERAN CHURCH**, Kandiyohi County
(beautiful lakeside church)
• **PIPESTONE NATIONAL MONUMENT**, Pipestone
(ancient place of awe and inspiration)
• **SAINT CORNELIA'S EPISCOPAL CHURCH**, Redwood Falls
(Native American influence, with repatriation grounds nearby)
• **SAINT JOHN'S ABBEY**, Collegeville (award-winning architecture,
including a spectacular stained-glass window)

ꝶATIVE ꝶMERICAN ꝶITES

Pipestone National Monument

At an ancient time the Great Spirit, in the form of a large bird, stood upon the wall of rock and called all the tribes around him, and breaking out a piece of the red stone formed it into a pipe and smoked it, the smoke rolling over the whole multitude. He then told his red children that this red stone was their flesh, that they were made from it, that they must all smoke to him through it, that they must use it for nothing but pipes; and as it belonged alike to all tribes, the ground was sacred, and no weapons must be used or brought upon it.

—Dakota account of the origin of the pipestone, as recorded by George Catlin, 1836

Pipestone National Monument is one of the most important Native American sites in the world. It is believed the Great Spirit created humankind here, and pipestone, the red stone common to the area, is our ancestors' hardened flesh and blood from the great flood. For centuries the location has been a place of peaceful pilgrimage for various tribes; they would travel up to 1,000 miles, on horseback and on foot, to obtain the stone they believed had been promised to them by the Creator.

Although the legend of the creation and the flood figures heavily in Native American lore about the red stone, there are other explanations as well. The

Omaha and Yankton Dakota believed that Wahegela, the Omaha wife of a Yankton Dakota, found the pipestone while trailing buffalo. The Omaha claimed the area because Wahegela was Omaha, but the Yankton claimed it because she lived and died among them. Finally the ground was considered holy and neutral. Another legend, retold by Longfellow in "Song of Hiawatha," said that the Great Spirit calls all nations together there, bidding them to live as brothers or they would all perish. To bind the truce, he demonstrated how to carve peace pipes out of the stone. This myth is dramatized each summer at the local Hiawatha Pageant.

Pipestone calumet pipes have been—and still are—highly prized by many Native American tribes to solemnize various occasions, to bind agreements, and for religious ceremony. Over time, the pipes evolved from simple tubes to more complex shapes and animal effigies, such as turtles, which symbolized long life. Made in many styles, shapes, and designs, the pipes are considered the primary means of communication between human beings and spiritual powers. Some Native Americans consider the pipe an altar, with the smoke carrying prayers to the Great Spirit.

Archaeological evidence shows that stone pipes were in use 2,000 years ago and that, over time, this location became the preferred location for getting the soft, pink-to-red stone. The French explorer and cartographer Joseph Nicollet visited the area in 1838 and carved his initials into the rock. In his journal, he wrote: "In the opinion of the Sioux [Dakota], who are fond of the marvelous, this quarry was opened by the Great Spirit of thunder, and one cannot visit it without being greeted by his rumblings and the lightning and storms that accompany them. We are able to testify on our part of the truth of this tradition, or at least our experience accorded with it. We were not one-half mile from the valley of thunder when lightning and heavy rain burst upon us."

Nicollet wrote that the Dakota prayed, fasted, and purified themselves for days before visiting the quarry, so that the spirit of the quarry "will let them have good stone which will not flake and is clear and compact and uniform." Impressed by his experience with the Native Americans there, he wrote, "Nothing equals the reserve and discretion of these good people. I cannot conceive why so many whites blunder in their dealings with them . . . a little tobacco and a few [kind] words will do what an army cannot do."

Since the official opening of the national monument in 1937, only those of Native American ancestry can quarry the redstone according to law. A total of 37 tribes are currently listed as having permits to quarry the pipestone, including Cheyenne, Comanche, Dakota, Inuit, and Ojibwe. Only hammers and chisels are allowed as tools in the ancient pits.

The Oracle Stone at Pipestone National Monument

Other sacred spots in the area include a grouping of enormous granite boulders called "The Three Maidens," which at one time were surrounded by a circle of petroglyphs. In addition, the Circle Trail, a self-guided path that takes about 45 minutes and features many grandfather and grandmother rocks, the Oracle Stone, "Leaping Rock," and Winnewissa Falls.

The nonprofit Pipestone Indian Shrine Association, acting as a cooperating association to the National Park Service, is dedicated to preserving the art form of pipemaking. All proceeds from book and craftwork sales are used to support historical, scientific, and educational activities of this national monument, which is on the National Register of Historic Places.

Two sun dances (week-long celebrations of ceremony, prayer, and dancing) are held annually at the site—the Yankton Sioux (Dakota) Tribe Sun Dance at the beginning of July and the Gathering of the Sacred Pipes Sun Dance the third week in August.

Call ahead for hours and fees.

Located at 36 Reservation Avenue (one mile north of town off Highway 75), Pipestone, Pipestone County; (507) 825-5464; www.nps.gov/pipe

The "Three Maidens" at Pipestone National Monument

Equinox Rock Line

No one knows who built this 1,250-foot line of rocks in what is now Blue Mounds State Park, but it is clearly of human origin. Sunrise and sunset are perfectly aligned along the rock line on the spring and fall equinox. Some people have speculated that the rocks are a "road marker for space aliens." The rock line, sometimes hidden by brush and plant growth, is located off the Burr Oak Trail near the park's interpretive center, along the park's southern perimeter. Nearby is Eagle Rock, a spiritually important landmark. At 300 feet, it's the highest hill in the park. Blue Mounds is home to the largest herd of bison in the state.

The park was named for a 1,000-foot cliff of pipestone (also known as Sioux quartzite). It is on the National Register of Historic Places and on the list of federal and state protected sites. The interpretive center is open May through September.

Located in Blue Mounds State Park, six miles north of Luverne off Highway 75; (507) 283-4892.

Jeffers Petroglyphs

More than 2,000 carvings of nearly 200 different objects appear on the surface of an outcropping of red quartzite 700 feet long and 150 feet wide in Cottonwood County. The Jeffers Petroglyphs, as the carvings are now called, show animals, abstract spirits, stick figures, and more. According to the Minnesota Office of Tourism, "The glyphs served many functions, including recording important events, depicting sacred ceremonies, and emphasizing the importance of animals and hunting." Some believe the images were used in special rituals—such as vision quests or hunting magic ceremonies—perhaps by more than one tribe.

Additional groups of rock carvings have been discovered in the area as far out as 23 miles from the Jeffers Petroglyphs Historic Site, but most of the others cannot be seen because they are on isolated or private land. The entire site contains the largest known concentration of petroglyphs in Minnesota.

Visitors can pick up a guidebook to self-guided trails at the tepee-shaped interpretive center. The visibility of the images varies, depending on the weather, angle of viewing, and time of day. The historic site is open from Memorial Day through Labor Day.

Located near Bingham, three miles east of Highway 71 on County Highway 10, then one mile south on County Highway 2; (507) 628-5591; jefferspetroglyphs@mnhs.org

Buffalo Ridge

The tip of this ridge is more than 1,900 feet above sea level, making it one of the highest points in the state. It has religious significance for the Dakota. Several rock outlines made by early Native Americans remain, and a Dakota smoke pit is at the summit. A Native American burial ground stands near the top. A very large silhouette of a bison, which can be seen for miles, has been installed at the apex of the ridge. Most of the ridge sits on a privately owned ranch. The bison silhouette is clearly visible along Highway 30. To visit the actual site, please contact the State Archaeologist's office (for contact information, see "A Note about the Preservation of Sacred Places" at the beginning of the book).

The Buffalo Ridge bison silhouette is about 11 miles east of Pipestone on Highway 30.

Upper Sioux Indian Community

This reservation along the Minnesota River, a few miles southeast of Granite Falls, represents one of the few remaining reservation tracts of the Upper Sioux (Dakota) Sisseton-Wahpeton, who were expelled from their tribal lands after the Dakota War of 1862. The reservation tracts were restored in the 1930s under the Indian Reorganization Act. A large Dakota burial mound sits across the road from the adjacent Upper Sioux Agency State Park. It is a testament to the Dakota that gave up their lives in their struggle to preserve their land.

Upper Sioux Agency State Park is eight miles southeast of Granite Falls on Highway 67; (320) 564-4777. The Wood Lake Historic Site, which marks the location of the last battle of the Dakota War, is 10 miles farther south, off Highway 67. For more information, contact the Upper Sioux Indian Community at P.O. Box 147, Granite Falls, MN 56241; (320) 564-2360.

Mdewakanton Repatriation and Reburial Site

Located within the Lower Sioux Indian Reservation, this gated shrine with protective sage medicine circles and recent offerings stands in memory of the Mdewakanton Dakota remains that were finally returned to their tribal lands after 125 years. The reburial grounds here and Saint Cornelia's Episcopal Church (see the "Episcopal Churches" section later in this chapter) are hallowed ground. A plaque from the Minnesota Historical Society describes the history of the exile and the efforts to restore the grounds. Many of the remains were brought from South Dakota and Nebraska. Some, such as the remains of Chief Mapiya Oki Najin (Cut Nose), which had been used for medical research, were hard to recover, but his remains are finally at rest in his ancestral home. Many others still await repatriation and proper burial. The site also features the remnants of the Lower Sioux Agency and an Interpretive Center. There are unmarked trails through the 140 acres of grasslands. Call ahead for visiting hours.

Located nine miles east of Redwood Falls, off County Highway 2.
For more information, contact the Lower Sioux Indian Community,
Route 1, Box 308, Morton, MN 56270;
(507) 697-6185 or (507) 697-6321.

Indian Point

Numerous artifacts, bison bones, ancient campsites, and petroglyphs have been found on this conical point in Flandreau State Park. Visitors can take self-guided interpretive tours.

Located at 1300 Summit Avenue, New Ulm; (507) 354-3519.

Minnewaska Burial Mound

According to legend, this is the burial ground of Princess Minnewaska, wife of the Ojibwe Chief White Bear. When the Dakota attacked the Ojibwe where the community of Glenwood now lies, Chief White Bear captured Minnewaska, the daughter of Pau-Wating, a Dakota warrior. Pau-Wating was killed and Minnewaska became Chief White Bear's wife. The lake that the burial mound overlooks, previously named White Bear Lake, was renamed Minnewaska in her honor. It is said that White Bear is buried beside her.

Located on County Highway 24, three miles west of Glenwood in
Pope County.

Mountain Lake Powwow Grounds

A powwow celebration is held here the third Monday and Tuesday in June each year. It is Minnesota's oldest continuing community celebration. The grounds and its structures are on the National Register of Historic Places.

Located at Mountain Lake (45 miles southwest of Mankato),
Cottonwood County.

Ish-tak-ha-ba Monument

Ish-tak-ha-ba, also known as Sleepy Eye, was a chief of the Sisseton Dakota and was known as a "friend to all men." The village and lake were named after him in 1872. His grave features a granite obelisk monument and a statue of the chief.

*Located on First Avenue at the train depot in Sleepy Eye
(about 13 miles west of New Ulm), Brown County.*

Mount Tom

The Dakota held this mountain, with an elevation of 1,375, in high spiritual regard. When clouds gathered close to the mountain, it reminded them of smoke from their sacred pipes, used in ceremonies. The trail starting north of the campground can be challenging, but the scenic views make it worth the effort.

Located in Sibley State Park, 800 Sibley Park Road NE (15 miles north of Willmar on Highway 71), New London; (320) 354-2055.

ℒUTHERAN ℐITES
Churches

Mamre Free Lutheran Church

In the 19th century, John Rodman, who settled on land northwest of Willmar, named the area Mamre, from the biblical reference to the home of Abram (later known as Abraham) in the Promised Land. Along with Rodman, Reverend J.P. Lundblad helped found the small community. Built in the late 19th century, the church, which sits along Church Lake, features Swedish and English signage, such as "frutten Gud och gif homonave" ("Praise God and Give Him Honor").

Located at 8500 75th Avenue, Church Lake, Kandiyohi County. From Willmar, take Highway 71 north about five miles to County Highway 27, and turn west following the highway around Long Lake about seven miles to County Highway 116. Turn left (south) and follow the road to 75th Avenue. The church is just past the mailboxes facing the lake.

Norway Lake Lutheran Churches

Enough Norwegians had settled in northwest Kandiyohi County by the late 1800s to require three churches. The East Norway Lake congregation, founded in 1862, was technically established first, but the West Norway Lake congregation formed the same year. West's current building, built in 1898, is the newest of the three buildings. The East and West congregations' church buildings are still used occasionally. The First Lutheran Church is now a merged congregation. Its 1893 building is the base of congregational activity in the area and is used more often than the other two churches. All three churches work in close cooperation.

The three churches are located near the tiny community of Norway Lake, Kandiyohi County. West Norway Lake Church is located at 68th Street NW and 165th Avenue NW. The First Lutheran Church was rebuilt on Highway 40 at Highway 1, with a view of the East Norway Lake Church, which is on County Highway 101 south of Highway 40.

East Norway Lake Lutheran Church, Kandiyohi County

Hadley Lutheran Church

Also known as Beaver Creek Church, this building is home to the oldest Lutheran congregation in Murray County; the church was founded in 1873. The congregation erected their first church building in 1880, and they constructed a new building, which still stands, 28 years later.

Located in the small community of Hadley (five miles west of Slayton), Murray County; (507) 836-6727.

First Lutheran Church

A model of a Viking ship hangs from the ceiling in the middle of the First Lutheran Church in Renville. The ship, a miniature likeness of the real thing, represents the Ark and the Church—both instruments of salvation. The ship is modeled after the "Norska Love" (Norwegian Lion), a ship used by Norwegian immigrants during the late 18th and early 19th century. The Norska Love is considered one of the most beautiful sailing ships ever built. Because the sea was such an integral part of people's lives in Scandinavia, many such ships are displayed in

Scandinavian churches (see also the Stavkirke description in chapter 4.)

In addition, the church features some stunning stained-glass images of the sacraments, a beautiful "Living Garden" outdoor chapel, and a meditation garden with a driftwood cross. A stone at the entry quotes Psalm 90: "Lord, thou hast been our dwelling place in all generations. Before the mountains were brought forth, or ever thou hast formed the earth and the world, from everlasting to everlasting, thou art God."

Located at Third Street SW and Dogwood Avenue, Renville, Renville County; (320) 329-3954.

The Living Garden at the
First Lutheran Church, Renville

Westerheim Icelandic Lutheran Church/ Saint Paul's Evangelical Lutheran Church

Saint Paul's Evangelical Lutheran Church congregation was founded in 1887, and the building and parsonage are on the National Register of Historic Places. An 1895 article in a local paper had this to say: "The Icelandic Church at this place is now finished. . . . The pews and pulpit have been purchased by the Ladies Aid Society for $260 and the chandeliers by the young ladies for $55. The total cost of the church when finished and totally furnished as contemplated will exceed $3,000. This structure adds greatly to our pretty village, and will, we hope, prove a potent factor in the maintenance and promotion of Christianity and morality among us."

In 1955, the congregation of nearby Westerheim Icelandic Lutheran Church, founded in 1881, merged with Saint Paul's because of declining enrollments. Westerheim's beautiful building collapsed while being moved in 1964.

Located at 412–414 East Lyon Street, Minneota (about 10 miles northwest of Marshall), Lyon County; (507) 872-6605.

Danebod Lutheran Church

Founded in 1885 by Danish immigrants, this church is considered an architectural jewel and is on the National Register of Historic Places. The exterior of the church has been repaneled but its unique architecture has been maintained. The interior contains many historic items. The church is part of the town of Tyler's Danebod Historical Complex, which also includes a folk school patterned after those in Denmark, a gym, and a stone hall. Tyler is known as the "Home of the Nissemaend," tiny elves that are said to occupy Danish homes. These creatures are like leprechauns—no one ever sees them. If the homeowner lays out food for them, they can be helpful; if not, they can be mischievous.

Located at 101 Danebod Court, Tyler, Lincoln County; (507) 247-5344; danebod@mnns.com.

Danebod Lutheran Church, Tyler

Hawk Creek Evangelical Lutheran Church

In the 1870s, the Reverend E. M. Eriksen served several Lutheran congregations in and around the community of Sacred Heart. After much discussion, a united church was built in 1880, and the Western Hawk Creek congregation and the Norwegian-Danish Evangelical Lutheran congregation merged to form Hawk Creek Evangelical Lutheran Church. Over time, several other congregations, including Sacred Heart Church, also merged with Hawk Creek.

Located on County Road 60 at 130th Street, Sacred Heart,
Renville County; (320) 765-2782.

Hawk Creek Evangelical Lutheran Church,
Renville County

Why "Sacred Heart"?

In 1783, Charles Patterson opened a trading post in the northwestern part of what later was designated Renville County. He was given the Native American nickname of "sacred hat man" for wearing a bearskin hat (bears are sacred animals to many Native American tribes). Somehow, "sacred hat" evolved into "sacred heart," and that became the name of the nearby town, an interesting situation given that the town is largely Lutheran. Nearby Sacred Heart Creek got its name from yet another source—the mouth of the creek had formed into the shape of a heart. Established in the 1850s, the Sacred Heart Mission, named for the creek, served "half-breeds and Indians" and was overseen by a French missionary. The church at the site of the mission is long gone; its congregation was one of several that merged to form the Hawk Creek Evangelical Lutheran Church.

East Union Lutheran Church

Local farmers built this yellow-brick building in 1866 as a testament of faith. Their community was one of the earliest Swedish settlements in Minnesota.

Located at 15255 County Highway 40 (at County Highway 50), East Union, Carver County; (952) 448-3450.

Other Sites

Gustavus Adolphus College

Founded in 1862 by Swedish Lutheran immigrants, the college, which is on the National Register of Historic Places, overlooks the city of Saint Peter and the Minnesota River Valley. The school's 55-acre arboretum is an oasis of plants from all regions of Minnesota and features a white garden and lilac grove. Self-guided tours and a map of campus are available, and guided tours can be arranged. The focal point of the campus is Christ Chapel, an ultramodern chapel that features a dramatic curtain wall and a rapier-thin spire. The chapel is connected with the Norseland Lutheran Church, founded in Saint Peter in 1858.

The college is located at 800 West College Avenue, Saint Peter, Nicollet County; (507) 933-7550.

Green Lake Lutheran Ministries Bible Camp

Established in 1938, this camp sits on 62 acres along the south shore of Green Lake. It features a historic chapel modeled after Norwegian staved churches. An independent Lutheran board runs the camp. The camp can accommodate up to 200 people.

Located at 9916 Lake Avenue South, Spicer, Kandiyohi County; (320) 796-2181; www.gllm.org

Chi Rho Center

Saint John's Lutheran Church in Minneapolis operates this 76-acre retreat center on Lake Sylvia, south of Saint Cloud. Established in 1967, the facility is ecumenical and can serve groups of up to 44. Advance registration is necessary.

Located at 15759 55th Street NW, Annandale, Wright County; (320) 274-8307; www.chirhocenter.org

Martin Luther College

The college, run by the Wisconsin Evangelical Lutheran Synod College, sits atop a hill overlooking New Ulm. A bronze statue of Martin Luther watches over all who enter the campus. The main building, built in 1884, is on the National Register of Historic Places.

Located at 1995 Luther Court, New Ulm; (507) 354-8221; www.mlc-wels.edu

Shetek Lutheran Ministries Bible Camp

Shetek Lutheran Ministries Bible Camp has been located on Keeley Island in Lake Shetek since the 1940s. The Evangelical Lutheran Church in America retreat accommodates up to 20 couples or 180 youth. Youths attend camp here during the summer, and some public camping is available. The camp's Lakota Retreat Center has meeting rooms, as well as lodging accommodations. Reservations are required.

Located at 154 Keeley Island Drive, Slayton, Murray County;
(507) 763-3567; www.shetek.org; slbc@rconnect.com

CATHOLIC SITES
Cathedrals

Church of the Sacred Heart, Heron Lake

Church of the Sacred Heart

This magnificent neo-Baroque church was built 1921, patterned on Catholic churches in Germany and Austria. It was built on a basilica plan and features twin bell towers that soar above the prairie. A massive structure, it reflects the vision of church members who raised the funds to build it. The church's stained-glass windows, purchased from Franz Bisfield and Company of Trier, Germany, depict the sacraments and the Ten Commandments. Murals show the figures of Christ, Moses, and John the Baptist; sacred sites in Rome and the Holy Land; nearby buildings in Minnesota; people of faith; and the symbols of the four Evangelists who wrote the Gospels (Matthew is a human body; Mark is a Lion's head; Luke is an ox head; and John is an eagle head). The church is on the National Register of Historic Places.

Located at 321 Ninth Street, Heron Lake, Jackson County (about 18 miles northeast of Worthington); (507) 831-3300.

Cathedral of Saint Mary

In 1855, Father Francis Xavier Pierz founded this parish in a log church. The next year, a Benedictine priest became the parish's first pastor. The church's next building, of Gothic design, was built in 1864 and burned down in 1920. The current building was completed in 1931. It was designated the cathedral of the Saint Cloud Diocese in 1937, replacing Holy Angels Cathedral. In 1978, the interior was remodeled to follow guidelines from "Environment and Art in Catholic Worship," a document by the Bishop's Committee on the Liturgy that provides principles for those involved in preparing liturgical space.

Located at 25 South Eighth Avenue (at Saint Germain Street), Saint Cloud; (320) 251-1840; www.stmarysstcloud.org

Cathedral of the Holy Trinity

In 1866, parishioners laid the cornerstone for the first church building to occupy this site in New Ulm. After it was destroyed by a tornado in 1881, the congregation promised to say the Rosary every Saturday for protection from bad weather, a promise they have kept to this day. The congregation dedicated a new church building in 1893. Local artist Alexander Schwendinger provided the interior decorations, which were completed eight years later. In 1957, the church became the new cathedral of the New Ulm Diocese. An angel garden, between the church and the parish offices, was dedicated to the memory of deceased loved ones in 1997.

The cathedral's floor plan is similar to that of early Roman basilicas, with rounded arches of Romanesque architecture resting on heavy pillars. There is also a German Baroque influence in the interior décor, done in dark colors and with gold ornamentation. A beautiful mural of the Holy Trinity hangs above the altar, showing the Father with hands stretching out through symbols of the zodiac. Jesus is seated below the Father with his right hand in blessing, and a dove, representing the Holy Spirit, sits between them. Mary and her mother Anne are also depicted, as are cherubim that were painted in the likeness of children from the parish. The 12 apostles are shown around the apse. Saints are painted on the walls throughout. The bell tower and its four clock faces can be seen for miles.

Located at 605 North State Street, New Ulm; (507) 354-4158; www.cathedralht.org; newulmcathedral@hotmail.com

Mural in the Cathedral of the Holy Trinity, New Ulm

Historic Churches

Church of the Sacred Heart

The first Church of the Sacred Heart building in Freeport was dedicated in 1882, but it was replaced with a larger structure in 1898. This church, however, was destroyed by fire just six years later, and the present structure, on the National Register of Historic Places, was built in 1906. The archway above the sanctuary reads: "Sieh da dieses Herz, das die Menschen so sehr geliebt hat" ("Behold this Heart, He loved man so much").

Located at 106 Third Avenue NE, Freeport, Stearns County; (320) 836-2143.

Saint Mary, Help of Christians Church

This 1873 church, built by German immigrants a few miles south of Saint Cloud, has beautifully carved wooden altars. The original mission cross graces the front of the church, which is on the National Register of Historic Places.

Located at 24588 County Highway 7, Saint Augusta, Stearns County; (320) 252-1799.

Stearns County—Plenty of Catholic Churches

In addition to the historic Stearns County Catholic churches mentioned in the text, many more grace the area. All of the following except Saint Nicholas are on the National Register of Historic Places.

• **SAINT STEPHEN**, erected in 1880, 103 Central Avenue South (County Highway 2), Saint Stephen; (320) 251-1520.
• **SAINT JOSEPH**, built in 1874, 12 West Minnesota Street (at College Avenue), Saint Joseph; (320) 363-7505.
• **IMMACULATE CONCEPTION**, built in 1900, 37186 County Road 9, Saint Anna; (320) 356-7313.
• **SAINT BONIFACE** (also known as Saint Mary's), erected in 1875, 211 South Fifth Avenue East, Melrose; (320) 256-4207.
• **SAINT NICHOLAS**, 15862 County Highway 165, Watkins; (320) 764-7345.
• **SAINT ANTHONY** is the church that inspired Garrison Keillor's fictional Our Lady of Perpetual Responsibility in his mythical town of Lake Wobegon. It is located at 24328 Trobec Street, Saint Anthony; (320) 845-2416.
• **SEVEN DOLORS CHURCH** houses the statue of the Seven Dolors (Seven Sorrows), which was originally in Bolivia. It is now in the side chapel of the Sorrowful Mother. This 1872 30-by-60-foot wood-frame church has a tower and altar built in 1878. Located at 151 Second Street South, Albany; (320) 845-2708.

Church of Saint Michael

This church was constructed in 1890 in the town of the same name northwest of the Twin Cities. The German settlers founded the town in 1856. The church, on the National Register of Historic Places, features beautiful statuary with German woodcarvings.

Located at 22 Main Street, Saint Michael, Wright County; (763) 497-2745; www.churchofsaintmichael.org

Saint Thomas Catholic Church

This church was erected in 1870, replacing previous structures built in 1855 and 1862. The majestic building was the nucleus of the first Irish agrarian settlement in the state, which has since faded away.

Located five miles north of Henderson on County Highway 6, Sibley County.

Japanese Martyrs Catholic Church

In the middle of the 19th century, Commodore Matthew Perry entered Japan and began bringing news of that country to the West. It was learned that the Christian faith, despite two centuries of intolerance, was not dead. In 1865, 20,000 Christians were discovered practicing their religion in secret at Kiushu, Japan. At least 3,404 had suffered exile or prison for their faith; 660 of these had died, and 1,981 returned to their homes. In 1858, 112 Christians, among whom were two Jesuit chief-baptizers, were put to death by torture. One missionary calculates that 1,200 died for the Christian faith in Japan during this period. In 1862, they were declared saints by the Vatican. This church, in the tiny community of Leavenworth, was established in their name five years later. It is traditional in the Catholic Church to name new churches after recently canonized saints.

Located at 30881 County Highway 24, Leavenworth (about 25 miles southwest of New Ulm), Brown County; (507) 794-6974; jmartyrs@sleepyeyetel.net

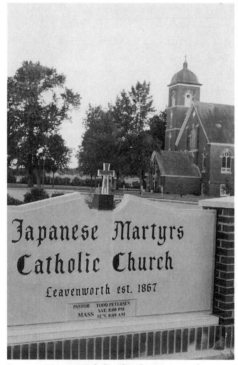

Japanese Martyrs Catholic Church, Leavenworth

Saint Mary's Church

Erected in 1886, this Gothic cathedral features two large towers. The church high school is across the street.

Located at First Avenue North and Saint Mary's Street NE, Sleepy Eye, Brown County; (507) 794-4171.

Shrines

Assumption Chapel

In the 1870s, when hordes of grasshoppers devoured precious crops in the area, local farmers began to pray fervently for divine intervention. After their prayers were answered, Father Leo Winter dedicated and built this chapel. Construction began in 1877, and, after it was completed, parishioners held a mass of thanksgiving every year for 15 years. This "Grasshopper Chapel," as it was called, was destroyed by a tornado in 1894. It wasn't rebuilt until 1952; utilizing the original foundation stones, the congregation erected the new building and renamed it Assumption Chapel. Over the entrance is an image of Mary and the words "Assumpta est Maria" ("Mary has been taken up to heaven").

The chapel is made of pink-gray granite, and the ceiling is California redwood. The interior walls are polished agate and carnelian. Stained-glass windows depict scenes in Mary's life, and the chapel houses a statue of Mary carved by the Slovenian artist Joseph Ambroziz. Visitors have made pilgrimages to the church from all over the world. In fact, the earliest recorded religious pilgrimages to Minnesota were to this shrine. Since 1990, about 400 people per week have attended novena masses on Thursday evenings to pray for good harvests.

Just outside the chapel is a shrine to Saint Joseph and an outdoor Way of the Cross, which is illuminated so it can be visited 24 hours a day.

Located on the outskirts of Cold Spring (about 15 miles southwest of Saint Cloud) on Highway 23, Stearns County; (320) 685-3280; www.ohwy.com/mn/a/asptchap.htm

Assumption Chapel, Cold Spring

95

Another "Grasshopper Shrine"

During the same grasshopper invasion of the 1870s that inspired the building of the "Grasshopper Chapel," the people of the nearby towns of Luxemburg and Saint Augusta made a similar pledge. The result was a shrine to Saint Boniface, and every June 5, the local faithful would make a pilgrimage to it by foot. But their later generations didn't follow suit, and eventually the chapel was abandoned and has slowly deteriorated.

Saint Boniface Parish

This parish was established in 1878. The new modern sanctuary has a 10-to-12-foot-tall icon shrine to Mary in traditional Byzantine style. The parish is not related to the Saint Boniface shrine in the sidebar.

Located at 418 Main Street, Cold Spring; (320) 685-3280; www.stboniface.com; st.boniface@juno.com

Our Lady of Victory Shrine

This is an isolated shrine at the location of a former church. It features a statue of Mary, which is surrounded by cedars and a memorial plaque. It is situated on the only hill in the area.

Located south of Highway 19 on County Highway 5 near 250th Street, Redwood County.

Our Lady of Victory Shrine, Redwood County

Schoenstatt Shrine and Retreat Center

Erected in 1976, the Schoenstatt Center, near Sleepy Eye, is one of seven Schoenstatt shrines in the United States, and one of more than 160 worldwide. They are all exact replicas of the original shrine located in Schoenstatt, Germany, near Coblenz.

Founded by the Reverend J. Kentenich, who died in 1968, the shrines are dedicated to Mother Thrice Admirable, Queen and Victress of Schoenstatt. Waukesha, Wisconsin, has the oldest Schoenstatt Shrine in the United States; it was dedicated in 1964. Thousands of pilgrims visit the shrines each year. The organization says visitors will "escape from the anxious restlessness of the present age and attach [themselves] to a place where [they] feel loved and accepted." Faithful visitors to the shrines are said to be rewarded with three main graces: "devotion to God, inner transformation in Christ, and apostolic fruitfulness."

Among the special features of each of the intimate chapels are a specially designed crucifix, an ornately carved altar, and Schoenstatt's Picture of Grace (a painting of Jesus and Mary). In addition to the Minnesota and Wisconsin shrines, there are also U.S. shrines in Texas and New York.

Located on Highway 14 West, Sleepy Eye, Brown County;
(507) 794-5622 or (507) 794-7727.

Way of the Cross

In 1904, this shrine was built in New Ulm by the Sisters of the Poor Handmaids of Jesus Christ, who owned and managed Loretto Hospital and Saint Alexander Home for the aged (which is now the New Ulm Medical Center). Set along a path on a hill leading up from the medical center, the shrine has 14 stations, featuring Bavarian statuary, that portray the agony and crucifixion of Christ. Midway uphill is a shrine to Our Lady of Lourdes. At the summit is a chapel dedicated to Our Sorrowful Mother. The shrine site affords visitors a marvelous view of New Ulm and the Minnesota River Valley.

Located behind the New Ulm Medical Center between Highland Avenue and Garden Street, New Ulm.

Shrine of the Divine Mercy

This shrine, housed inside Saint Paul's Church in Sauk Centre, honors Saint Faustina Kowalska, an uneducated Polish nun of the Congregation of the Sisters of Our Lady of Mercy, who was the source of the Devotion to the Divine Mercy. Saint Paul's is believed to be the first community in the United States dedicated to the Mercy of God of Sister Faustina.

The 600-page diary of Sister Faustina, entitled *Divine Mercy in My Soul,* describes the joy and suffering she felt while experiencing "God's revelations to her about His unfathomable mercy." She wrote in secret, with only her spiritual director and a few superiors aware of the visions and sufferings she was undergoing. Only after her death in 1938 did word of her great mystical experiences reach the outside world.

Saint Paul's was dedicated in April 1982. Among those in attendance was Maureen Digan of Stockbridge, Massachusetts, who had recovered from illness at the gravesite of Sister Faustina, a miracle that has been recognized by the Catholic Church. Saint Paul's also features a carving of the Merciful Jesus.

Saint Paul's Church is located at 304 Sinclair Lewis Avenue, Sauk Centre, Stearns County; (320) 352-2196; www.brendans-island.com/mercy.htm

Shrine of the Divine Mercy, St. Paul's Church, Sauk Center

Colleges and Retreat Centers

Saint Benedict's Monastery

Opened in 1857, Saint Benedict's is one of the largest Benedictine monasteries in the United States and most likely the largest community of Benedictine women in the world. It is adjacent to the campus of the College of Saint Benedict. The monastery has a retreat program called the Spirituality Center. The 1914 Romanesque chapel was renovated in 1983 and features a Noack organ, an oratory, and the Blessed Sacrament Chapel.

Located at 104 Chapel Lane, Saint Joseph, Stearns County; (320) 363-7100 (monastery) or (320) 363-7114 (Spirituality Center).

Christ the King Retreat Center

The Dakotas called this place Dabinawa, meaning "sheltered, quiet place." Today, resting on a bluff overlooking Buffalo Lake about 30 miles northwest of downtown Minneapolis, the site is overseen by the Ministry of Missionary Oblates of Mary Immaculate. A sign at the retreat center reads: "All who seek

God and wish to grow in their spiritual lives are invited to come and share in the gift of Dabinawa." The facilities, built in 1952, are open to not-for-profit groups and organizations. The retreat can serve up to 131 people, with well-equipped meeting rooms, small group rooms, a large conference room, and a spacious chapel. Regular silent retreats are offered.

Located at 621 South First Avenue, Buffalo, Wright County; (763) 682-1394; www.kingshouse.com; christtheking@kingshouse.com

Clare's Well

This "women's spirituality farm" and retreat center was inspired by Clare of Assisi, a 13th-century mystic and friend of Saint Francis. The retreat "calls on the Franciscan virtues of a loving respect for all creation, joyful hospitality and solidarity with the marginated." The converted 40-acre farm and lake wetlands is operated by Franciscan Sisters of Little Falls. It features an outdoor grass labyrinth, some hermitages, and facilities for small group retreats. The farm's motto is "Wisdom is simple and deep within. Drink from your own well." Call ahead and request a map for specific directions.

Located at 13537 47th Street, Annandale (approximately 25 miles south of Saint Cloud); (320) 274-3512; www.fslf.org/

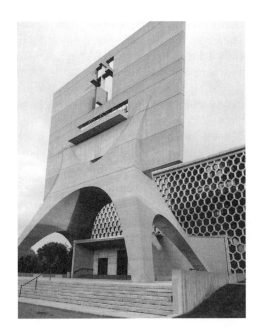

Saint John's Abbey

Located west of Saint Cloud, Saint John's Abbey, along with a university, occupies 2,400 acres around Lake Sagatagan and Strumpf Lake. Some 1,500 acres of the site is forestland, and the property is crisscrossed by 12 miles of hiking trails.

Benedictine monks from Saint Vincent Abbey in Pennsylvania came to the area in 1856 and built a school here. By 1860, after expanding the school, the monks were serving more than 50 communities in the area. The Abbey Church was designed by an Marcel Breuer, an Orthodox Jew whose design was chosen from 15 submissions. Completed in 1961, the church has won awards and worldwide attention for its design. Breuer also designed the library, science center, and other buildings.

The walls and ceiling of the church are made of corrugated, reinforced concrete. The huge structure seats close to 2,000, and its honeycombed stained-glass window is said to be the largest in the world. Designed by the late Branislaw Bak, a former member of the art department of Saint John's University, the glass suggests the splendor of the liturgical year, using brilliant bands of colored glass cut to various geometrical shapes. In the center is a unifying image of God expressed through a series of roughly concentric circles.

Visitors can take self-directed tours of the interior. They will find a bronze statue of Patron Saint John the Baptist, cast by Doris Caesar, near the baptistery in the front of the church. Downstairs are the crypt and chapel of Our Lady of the Assumption. On the back wall of the crypt is a separate shrine containing relics of many saints. In the main church, a Marian shrine contains a 12th-century woodcarving of the Madonna and Child; it was a gift from a friend of the abbey.

Outside the church there is a large white-oak cross, and a 2,500-ton concrete bell banner with five bells, which was dedicated on Christmas Day, 1989. The largest bell weighs more than 8,000 pounds. The bells are dedicated to the Holy Trinity, Blessed Virgin Mary, Guardian Angels, Saint John the Baptist, and Saint Benedict.

The Maris Stella Chapel, on a rocky point across Lake Sagatagan from the main campus, is a shrine honoring the Lady of the Lake. It is accessible by trail, but visitors must register.

Saint John's organizes group and private retreats through its Spiritual Life program. It also offers a Monastic Life program for men to live as monks for extended periods. The House of Prayer, a meditation chapel run by the Episcopal Church, is located on campus (see entry for the House of Prayer below).

Located on County Highway 159, 12 miles west of Saint Cloud. From I-94, take exit 156 near Collegeville. (320) 363-2011 or (320) 363-2573; www.saintjohnsabbey.org; spirlife@csbsju.edu

EPISCOPAL SITES

Episcopal Church of the Good Samaritan

Dedicated in 1869, the Episcopal Church of the Good Samaritan is the oldest church building in continuous use in Sauk Centre. A gift from a widow in New York who knew the first vicar and designer, Reverend George Stewart, covered the construction costs of the church. The parish erected a historical marker in 1987. The architecture is Gothic Revival, and the building features a 50-foot steeple corner.

Located on Sixth and Main Streets, Sauk Centre, Stearns County; (320) 352-6882.

Episcopal Church of the Good Samaritan,

Sauk Centre

House of Prayer

This meditation chapel on the grounds of Saint John's Abbey (see entry earlier in this chapter) "evokes an experience of solitude and an awareness of God's presence" with its award-winning design of wood, glass, and stone, as well as the surrounding forests with their miles of walking trails.

Saint John's Abbey is located on County Highway 159, 12 miles west of Saint Cloud. From I-94, take exit 156 near Collegeville. (320) 363-3293; houseofprayer@cloudnet.com

Saint Cornelia's Episcopal Church

Begun before the Dakota Conflict of 1862, this church—established by Saint John's Episcopal Mission to serve Christian members of the Dakota—remained unfinished. After the Dakota were forcibly resettled on reservations in other states, members of the Lower Sioux (Dakota) community gradually returned to the area. In 1862, the incomplete structure was dismantled and the stones moved to Saint Cornelia's present location. This Gothic Revival church, completed in 1891, was the center of Mdewakanton Dakota community life for several generations. There is a beautiful native star behind the altar cross. The structure is on the National Register of Historic Places.

Located off County Highway 2 on the Lower Sioux Indian Reservation, east of Redwood Falls, Redwood County.

Saint Cornelia's Episcopal Church, Lower Sioux Indian Reservation

Saint John's Episcopal Mission

The church was first built in Beaver Falls in 1891 and is now part of the Renville County Historical Museum complex in nearby Morton, having been moved there in 1997. There is a small admission charge for the museum. Call ahead for hours.

*Located at 441 North Park Drive, Morton, Renville County; (507) 697-6147;
www.rootsweb.com/~mnrenvil/mus-rchs.htm; rchs@rconnect.com*

Saint Paul's Episcopal Church

Although part of the Pope County Museum, this church is still used for
Sunday services. The interior and the exterior are original and in wonderful
condition. The church was originally in downtown Glenwood; parishioners
laid its cornerstone in 1893.

*Located at 809 South Lakeshore Drive, Glenwood, Pope County;
(320) 634-3293.*

*Saint Paul's Episcopal Church on the Pope County
Museum Grounds, Glenwood*

Church of the Good Shepherd

The church contains Minnesota's first stained-glass window, which was
made in Switzerland. This church was built in 1872 under the direction of
Bishop Henry Whipple and has remained unaltered. The pews are of wooden-
peg construction. Special services are held in the church throughout the year,
and it is available for weddings and other sacred events. The structure is on the
National Register of Historic Places.

*Located at Moore and Eighth Streets, Blue Earth, Faribault County. For more
information, contact the Wakefield House at (507) 526-5421.*

Church of Holy Communion Episcopal

Bishop C. Jackson Kemper conducted the first Episcopal service here in 1854. The current Gothic building was built in 1869. It's on the National Register of Historic Places.

Located at 116 North Minnesota Avenue, Saint Peter, Nicollet County; (507) 931-2542.

$\mathscr{O}$THER $\mathscr{C}$HURCHES AND $\mathscr{R}$ELATED $\mathscr{S}$ITES

Union Presbyterian Church

The merger of the First Free Presbyterian Church of Traverse de Sioux and the First Presbyterian Church of Saint Peter in 1869 formed one of the first union churches in Minnesota—Union Presbyterian Church. Both congregations were among the first Presbyterian congregations in the state. The present building, on the National Register of Historic Places, was erected in 1871. It features the original stained glass.

Located at 730 South Third Street, Saint Peter, Nicollet County; (507) 931-4602; www.spupc.org

Lac qui Parle Mission

Dr. Thomas S. Williamson and Joseph Renville founded this mission at the southeast end of Lac qui Parle Lake along the Minnesota River; many consider Lac qui Parle Mission Minnesota's first Protestant chapel, or the first church of the "new era." Renville, the son of a French fur trader and a Dakota woman, invited missionaries to settle in the area. (A trading post had been established there in 1826 at a long-standing Wahpeton Dakota village.)

Dakota women and parishioners built the church between 1938 and 1841; the mission had the first church bell in Minnesota. The Reverend Stephen Riggs, an early missionary, was the pastor of the church and translated the Bible into Dakota (he had also helped develop a Dakota alphabet). Also, as an advocate for peace 1850s, he worked to create a Native American nation in Minnesota in the 1850s, although the idea never gained wide support among European settlers.

The mission began to decline with the death of Renville. Eventually, the church burned down, and the site was abandoned. In the 1940s, a wooden chapel was built at the same site. Today, that site is open to the public, with several historical displays about the mission's efforts. There is a self-guided tour with interpretive signs. Admission is free.

Located on County Highway 13, eight miles northwest of Montevideo and three miles west of Highway 59, Chippewa County; (320) 269-7636.

Lac qui Parle Mission, Montevideo

Community United Methodist Church

Founded in the 1850s, this church, formerly known as the Simpson Methodist Episcopal Church, is on the National Register of Historic Places.

Located at 9225 Jason Avenue NE, Monticello, Wright County; (763) 295-2652.

Rough-Hewn Interior of the Lac qui Parle Mission

105

Koinonia Retreat Center

A ministry of Hennepin United Methodist Church in Minneapolis, this retreat provides opportunities for children, youth, and adults to grow at a "place apart." Established in 1964, the center is west of Annandale on Lake Sylvia.

Located at 7838 Pilger Avenue, South Haven, Wright County; (320) 236-7746; www.koinoniaretreatcenter.org

Children's Chapel

One of five buildings in the Laura Ingalls Wilder Museum complex, Children's Chapel is a former Methodist church that was moved to the site to be used as a place of ecumenical worship. A Congregational church provided the pews, a Catholic church the altar cloths, and a Lutheran church the window. Of special note is the "little red pew" from the original Union Congregational Church, which was made famous by Laura Ingalls Wilder (of "Little House" books fame), who lived behind the church with her family in 1875.

The Laura Ingalls Wilder Museum is located at 330 Eighth Street, Walnut Grove, Redwood County; (507) 859-2358; www.walnutgrove.org

Children's Chapel on the grounds of the Laura Ingalls Wilder Museum, Walnut Grove

Big Stone Farmer Cooperative

In 1956, the first Hutterite farming colony in Minnesota was established in the far western part of the state. The original 80-member colony moved from Ethan, South Dakota. Although Hutterites operate farms with modern machinery, they shun many modern conveniences and conventions, including cosmetics, contemporary clothing, and electronic equipment. Hutterites hold all property in common, believe that baptizing babies is not based on biblical precedent, and are pacifistic. They attend religious services almost every day.

Tour groups are welcome to visit the colony on any day except Sunday. No photographs of the colonists are allowed.

Located on Highway 28, Graceville, Big Stone County; (320) 748-7961.

Mennonite Heritage Village

This Mennonite village provides some fascinating glimpses into the past, with several buildings transplanted from the 1890s. Also featured are a large collection of historic phone equipment and a general store stocked as it would have been at the turn of the 20th century. Mennonite traditions are preserved in the restaurant named "Heritage Ayte Shtade" (literally, "eating place" in the Mennonite dialect of German) located in the village. The staff dresses accordingly and serves dishes like moos (a cold fruit soup), klups (a meatloaf patty with vegetables), and other Mennonite specialties. The village is open to the public summer evenings Thursday through Saturday and after noon on Sunday.

Located on County Highway 1 south of Highway 60, Mountain Lake,
Cottonwood County; (800) 794-6366; www.winwacc.com

Holy Myrrhbearers Orthodox Church in America

This Russian Orthodox Church in America church is in the former Grace United Methodist Church building. In the 1980s, the congregation worshipped next door in what is now the rectory before taking over the Methodist building.

Located at 601 Seventh Avenue South, Saint Cloud, Stearns County.

Clearwater Gospel Tabernacle

This Greek Revival structure, built in 1873 as the First Congregational Church, is now owned by the Clearwater Gospel Tabernacle. It is on the National Register of Historic Places.

Located at the intersection of Bluff and Elm Streets, Clearwater,
Wright County.

Morning Glory Meditation Gardens

Originally the work of Edward Barsness, these mediation gardens are now tended by various civic groups in Pope County. Barsness spent over 2,000 hours in 1965 cultivating this plot on the shore of Lake Minnewaska. After he died, his legacy continued in what has become a local tourist attraction. Except for Barsness's wish for people to enjoy the gardens, little else is known of his motivation. In 1981, the Challenge Ministry Chapel, built in 1970 on the other side of the lake, was moved to the gardens, where it is surrounded by more than 30 varieties of flowers. Many quotes grace the lovely surroundings: "What makes a garden and why do gardens grow—love lives in gardens God and lovers know" and "The dawn of the morning for glory, The hush of the night for peace, In the garden at eve says the story, God walks and his smile brings release."

Located on Highway 28 at North Ridge Drive, four miles west of Glenwood and five miles east of Starbuck in Pope County.

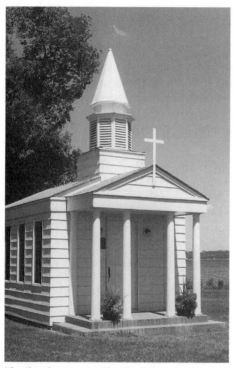

The Chapel at Morning Glory Mediations Gardens,
near Glenwood

Palmyra Covenant Church

Parishioners erected Palmyra Covenant Church in 1891. The congregation joined the Evangelical Covenant Churches of America in 1906. A quaint rural church, it is the oldest Covenant church in Minnesota. The roots of the Covenant Church are set in the Protestant Reformation and the Lutheran Church of Sweden, and the tenets of the church reflect spiritual awakenings of the 19th century.

Located at 44031 County Highway 4, Hector, Renville County;
(320) 848-2438.

Nora Unitarian Universalist Church

Built in 1881 as the Nora Free Christian Church, this large building and house are on the National Register of Historic Places.

Located at 12333 155th Avenue, Hanska (about 12 miles south of New Ulm), Brown County; (763) 439-6240; www.nora-uu-church.org/nora; norachuu@prairie.lake.com

Inside the Nora Unitarian Universalist Church, Hanska

Olof Swensson Farmstead Museum

Olof Swensson has been described as "peculiar," "a half century ahead of his time," a "genius," and a "fool." He emigrated from Norway in the 1870s and marketed Swensson's Flour until 1904. Around this time, he built a 22-room house at the present site of the museum. He became a religious advocate and preacher, conducting weekly religious services in the large chapel upstairs. His sermons have been preserved in Norwegian. The building is on the National Register of Historic Places.

Located on County Highway 15, about 12 miles southeast of Montevideo. For more information, contact the Chippewa County Historical Society, Montevideo; (320) 269-7636; CCHS.June@juno.com

*P*lenty of Hope in Southern Minnesota

Southern Minnesota is filled with Hope—there is the village of Hope in Steele County; a Hope Lake in Meeker County; a Hope Township in Lincoln County, south of Tyler. A former Native American village was located between Hope Lake and New Hope.

NORTHERN

Including the counties of Aitkin, Becker, Beltrami, Carlton, Cass, Clay,
Clearwater, Cook, Crow Wing, Douglas, Grant, Hubbard, Itasca, Kanabec,
Kittson, Koochiching, Lake, Lake of the Woods, Mahnomen, Marshall,
Mille Lacs, Morrison, Norman, Otter Tail, Pennington, Pine, Polk, Red Lake,
Roseau, Saint Louis, Todd, Traverse, Wadena, and Wilkin

CHAPTER 4
NORTHERN MINNESOTA

*Here Nature has been given a breathing space
and still heals men's minds and spirits
with the balm of her peace.*
—Grace Lee Nute, Rainy River Country

For Minnesotans, "Up North" isn't just a geological reference; it's a state of mind. Boundless forests and seemingly endless lakes connect the United States and Canada, with the Rainy River and International Falls along the border. Bodies of water are often considered sacred by many Native American tribes, and this region has hundreds of lakes, adding to the pristine beauty of Minnesota's North Woods.

Minnesota is full of "Spirit Lakes." Names of lakes, falls, rivers, and an island reflect Native American beliefs in spirits, especially belief in the Manitou, the Great Spirit. White settlers named other sites "Devil," a moniker that was a mistranslation of the word "Spirit."

Lake Superior—the largest body of freshwater in the world—has provided sustenance for Native Americans and European settlers alike. Known as Gichigummi (Gitchee Goome, or "Big Waters"), Lake Superior is the subject of many myths and legends. Along Minnesota's North Shore of Lake Superior, compasses malfunction when ships pass in the vicinity, due to huge amounts of iron ore in the shoreline cliffs; some 40 miles away, Magnetic Lake, with iron ore deposits in its lakebed, has similar effects.

Magnetism fascinated ancient peoples, who attributed its properties to spiritual forces. Practitioners of magic set up energy fields using magnetite to block out negative vibrations; they believed that placing a small piece of the rock into the ear would allow them to hear the voices of deities. Other magical uses of magnetic rock have included the attraction of love, the healing of illness, the drawing of pain from the body, the improvement of sexual relations, and the improvement of relationships.

The forests of northern Minnesota were home to the Dakota until the 16th century, when—after a long period of peace—the Ojibwe, in a long series of wars, forced the Dakota onto the prairies west of the Mississippi. The Ojibwe held claim to northeast Minnesota until they ceded the territory to the United States in 1854. In the 18th and early 19th centuries, Catholic and Protestant missionaries were among the primary European inhabitants. In the mid-19th century, Father Francis Xavier Pierz, a missionary from the Austro-Hungarian Empire, founded the first Catholic church in central Minnesota, and many Lutheran congregations formed at this time as well.

Best of Northern Minnesota

- **ARC ECUMENICAL RETREAT CENTER**, Stanchfield
(intimate, interfaith source of spiritual renewal)
- **CATHEDRAL OF OUR LADY OF THE ROSARY**, Duluth
(beautiful building with a view of Lake Superior)
- **FORT SAINT CHARLES**, Magnusson Island
(a restored chapel on the site of one of the earliest chapels in the Northwest Angle)
- **GRAND MOUND**, International Falls
(largest burial mound in the upper Midwest)
- **HEGMAN LAKE PICTOGRAPHS**, Boundary Waters Canoe Area Wilderness (vivid display of early Native American rock paintings)
- **HOLY FAMILY CATHOLIC CHURCH**, Belle Prairie
(oldest Catholic church in central Minnesota)
- **KENSINGTON RUNESTONE**, Alexandria
(purportedly the site of a Viking prayer dating back to 1362)
- **LAKE ITASCA**, Itasca State Park
(headwaters of the Mississippi River, sacred to Native Americans)
- **SPIRIT ROCK ISLAND**, Mille Lacs Kathio State Park
(site of mysterious "moving island," sacred to the Dakota)
- **SPIRIT ISLAND**, Nett Lake
(site of 150 petroglyphs sacred to the Ojibwe)
- **OUR LADY OF THE HOLY ROSARY CHURCH**, Grand Portage
(well-preserved early Catholic site)
- **SAINT FRANCIS CENTER**, Little Falls
(home of the breathtaking Sacred Heart Chapel)

$\mathscr{N}$ATIVE $\mathscr{A}$MERICAN AND
$\mathscr{N}$ATURAL $\mathscr{S}$ITES
Arrowhead Region and the Lake Superior Shoreline

Manido Geezhi-gans ("Spirit Little Cedar")

This twisted white cedar has overlooked Lake Superior for three centuries, probably longer. Manido geezhi-gans (pronounced "ma-ni-do gee-shi-gance"), Minnesota's oldest living landmark, has always been honored—or feared. The Ojibwe say that a hawk-like bird spirit is trapped inside the tree and will cause canoes to be wrecked on rocks, unless the tree is appeased with tobacco. According to another legend, an evil spirit that possessed the tree was frightened away by the guns of white men. In the 20th century, whites named the tree "the Witch Tree." In 1989, the Grand Portage Band of Ojibwe purchased the property and closed the site to the public to protect the sacred tree. Since 1991, Grand Portage Lodge and Casino has provided guided tours. Although not visible from the North Shore Highway (Highway 61), the tree can be seen from ferryboats traveling between the mainland and Isle Royale National Park.

Located in Cook County at Hat Point off County Highway 17, 2.5 miles east of the Grand Portage stockade. For more information, contact Grand Portage Lodge and Casino, Grand Portage; (218) 475-2401.

Grand Portage National Monument

One of the most historically significant and beautiful areas in all of Minnesota, the Grand Portage National Monument—near the Canadian border within the Grand Portage Indian Reservation—marks Minnesota's first permanent white settlement, founded in 1731. The monument is enclosed within Grand Portage Indian Reservation, where Ojibwe families have lived for hundreds of years. The name Grand Portage is translated from Kitchi Onigaming ("the Great Carrying Place").

In an unusual arrangement, the Ojibwe donated the site to the federal government in 1958 for use as a historic park; the national monument was established on January 27, 1960. Exhibits at the monument focus on the heritage of the Ojibwe and on their significant role in the fur trade of the 18th century. The business promoted international commerce and exploration in North America, as well as contact and cooperation between various Native American tribes and Northwest Company traders. Visitors to the monument will also find a reconstructed stockade, a great hall, a kitchen, and a warehouse.

The reservation covers the last 20 miles of Lake Superior shoreline before you reach the Canadian border, where there is a beautiful waterfall. At the wayside on Highway 61 near Grand Portage, you can view the Grand Portage harbor—and, on a clear day, Isle Royale National Park.

The Grand Portage Band of Ojibwe holds an annual "Rendezvous Days and Powwow Celebration." More than 300 Native American dancers participate, and attractions include "sights, sounds and aromas (that) take you back to the late 1700's." The powwow features traditional food, music, and crafts. Primitive camping is permitted in the monument.

The monument is a huge tourist draw—82,995 people visited in 2001, the last year that records are available. The grounds are open all year, with the heaviest tourism in July and August and lighter crowds from May to October. The stockade and buildings are open from late May to early October during regular business hours.

Grand Portage is 150 miles northeast of Duluth and 50 miles southwest of Thunder Bay, Ontario, along the north shore of Lake Superior. The national monument is located one mile south of Highway 61 on County Highway 17 in Grand Portage. For information, contact Grand Portage National Monument Headquarters 315 South Broadway, Grand Marais; (218) 387-2788; www.nps.gov/grpo.

Ojibwe Ni-Mi-Win Festival

Ojibwe people from throughout Minnesota and the Midwest gather for this annual event held near the Fond du Lac Reservation in Carlton and Saint Louis counties. The Ni-Mi-Win Festival is held the third weekend in August and features traditional Native American dancing. The specific location varies a bit from year to year, but the event is held at a location on the shore of Lake Superior. Fond du Lac is French for "bottom of the lake." The Ojibwe called the area Neg-adji-wanang, "the place where the water stops."

For information and location of the festival, call (800) 438-5884 or (218) 722-4011. The Fond du Lac Ojibwe Tribe can be reached at 105 University Road, Cloquet, MN 55720; (218) 879-4593; www.kstrom.net/isk/maps/mn/fondlac.htm.

Spirit Mountain

On September 15, 2001, spiritual leaders from the Bad River Reservation in Wisconsin followed the original migration of the Ojibwe People and walked to seven sacred stopping sites to fulfill prophecies, increase environmental awareness, and bring diverse communities together. The sixth of these stops was Spirit Mountain, an ancient site of vision quests and "sky burials" located just west of Duluth. There, the participants held a traditional Ojibwe "shaking tent" ceremony. They also revealed twelve burial sites on land marked for a proposed golf course. (The mountain is also the site of a popular ski resort.)

Nearby, Ely Peak was also the site of native vision quests and other coming-of-age ceremonies. Traditionally, a young male would climb to the summit and lie on a flat rock without food or water. After five days, his parents would bring him water to drink and then leave him for another five days. It's said that a gun-wielding "wild man" wearing a blue cap and red leggings protects those undergoing the ritual.

Another site is Bardon's Peak, named after a former landowner but known in native tongue as Manitoushgebik ("Spirit Mountain," not to be confused with the other Spirit Mountain nearby). According to legend, the spirit Naniboujou was said to live on the mountain. Possessed of enormous physical strength, he was thought to have created the Apostle Islands by throwing chunks of dirt at his rival Ah-Mik, the beaver spirit who dominated Gichigummi (Lake Superior). The western Duluth area is also known as Spirit Valley.

Spirit Mountain is located at 9500 Spirit Mountain Place, Duluth. Bardon's Peak is at 105th Avenue West and Skyline Drive, Duluth. Ely Peak is located just off Midway Road, about 2.5 miles south of Interstate 35 (exit 246), southwest of Duluth. For more information on the seven sacred stopping sites of the Ojibwe, see www.migrationjourney.cjb.net. For more information about the resort on Spirit Mountain, contact Spirit Mountain Recreation Area at (800) 642-6377 or (218) 628-2891, or www.spiritmt.com

Spirit Lake Village

A historic marker in John Astor City Park marks the place where the first peace treaty between the Ojibwe and the fur traders was signed at Spirit Lake Village, an Ojibwe community, in 1679.

Located at 133rd Avenue West at Evergreen Memorial Highway (Highway 23), Duluth.

Park Point (Shaga-Wa-Mik)

The world's longest river mouth sandbar—over six miles long—is situated where the Saint Louis River flows into Lake Superior. It is said to have been formed when the Great Spirit took pity on a trapped Ojibwe brave who was being chased by a Dakota band. He formed a sandy point in the cold waters to let the brave walk across to what is now Duluth without getting his moccasins wet, then caused the point to be swept into the bay. Shaga-wa-mik is Ojibwe for "long narrow point of land."

Located in the Duluth-Superior Harbor and accessible by car via the Duluth Aerial Life Bridge.

Spirits (and "Devils") in the North

Native Americans gave the name Manitou (and its alternate form Manido), or "spirit," to various natural attractions in Minnesota. White settlers simply used some form of the word "spirit" in much the same vein. Sometimes they considered Native American spirits evil, and so they used the word devils as an appellation for a number of other sites around the state. The northern area of Minnesota is rife with spirit-based names: Spirit Island, Spirit Valley, and Spirit Mountain, as well as Manitou Island, Manitou Rapids, Manitou Falls, and Manitou River. The Manido River flows from Lake Gratiot to White Fish Lake, near Jenkins in Crow Wing County.

MANITOU IN THE NORTH

In the Arrowhead region, the Manitou River drops 600 feet as it passes through the gorge in Crosby-Manitou State Park en route to Lake Superior. The dark and mysterious canyon has an enchanting, supernatural feel. Manitou Rapids, in Franz Jevne State Park, along the Rainy River, is the site of a sacred camp and the gravesites of great warriors and chiefs. Now a wayside, the park is on Highway 11 west of Grand Mound; you can see the rapids down the trail from the west parking area.

DEVIL'S CASCADE

The five-mile Devil's Cascade Trail ascends a steep ridge overlooking Lower Pawness Lake. If coming from the west, look for a sign just before the Little Indian Sioux River. It ends in a dramatic gorge with a beautiful waterfall with rock cairns. The trail is located in the Boundary Waters Canoe Area Wilderness, north of Lake Jeanette State Forest, about five miles north of Echo Trail (County Highway 116) on Forest Road 165.

DEVIL'S KETTLE WATERFALL

According to legend, the huge pothole at the bottom of the western division of the Brule River goes on and on forever. Dye, ping-pong balls, and even a car have been dropped in without ever having been seen again. Presumably, the pothole leads to another part of the river, but no one knows where. The trails near the pothole provide excellent views of Lake Superior. It is located at Judge C. R. Magney State Park, 18 miles northeast of Grand Marais in Cook County; (218) 387-2929 or (218) 226-3539.

LITTLE DEVIL'S RAVINE

This strange and unusual rock formation features a deeply cut canyon with many twists and turns. It's located near Pillsbury Peak, on Highway 210, about 22 miles west of Brainerd. For the exact location, ask for a Pillsbury State Forest map at the state forest district office in Pillager; (218) 746-4240.

DEVIL TRACK RIVER

The Ojibwe name for this sparkling stream is Manido bimadagakowini zibi ("Spirits' walking place on ice river"). The river runs behind Grand Marais (and old Chippewa City), and the area has splendid hiking for the seasoned hiker, with hidden waterfalls and canyons. The trail begins about one mile up the Gunflint Trail (County Highway 12) from Grand Marais.

Boundary Waters Canoe Area Wilderness

Every year, more than 160,000 tourists visit the Boundary Waters Canoe Area Wilderness along the Canadian border. Known as one of the most beautiful and well-preserved wilderness areas in the world, the BWCAW contains some of the oldest rock formations on earth. Geographically unique because of glacier activity that ended relatively recently (10,000 year ago), many parts of the area allow only canoes as transportation. Paddling enthusiasts will find more than 1,200 miles of navigable routes.

The BWCAW encompasses more than a million acres running some 200 miles along the Canadian border. The wilderness area is within the Superior National Forest, and Voyageurs National Park as well as Quetico Provincial Park (across the border in Ontario) are nearby. Although the BWCAW has been protected as a wilderness area since 1926, the current boundaries were set under the BWCA Wilderness Bill of 1978.

Magnetic Lake and Magnetic Rock

The area around mysterious Magnetic Lake contains large deposits of magnetite, causing compass needles to spin wildly. Native Americans believed the magnetism to be the result of spiritual energies. A 10-foot-wide, 20-foot thick, 30-foot-high natural monolith of magnetite stands on the shoreline, like one of the rocks of Stonehenge. Plan to spend much of the day at the lake to really see this site, but be careful—your compass could be damaged from prolonged exposure.

To reach Magnetic Lake by canoe, turn onto the Gunflint Trail (County Highway 12) in Grand Marais and follow it 45 miles northwest to County Highway 50, then turn right. Follow the hilly gravel road to Gunflint Lake. Magnetic Lake is straight across Gunflint Lake. To reach the lake on foot, follow the Gunflint Trail to the parking lot for the Kekebabic Trail, which is a few miles further north from the intersection with County Highway 50. The trailhead for the Magnetic Trail, a two-mile hiking path to the lake, is about a quarter mile north of the lot.

ℐome "Holy" Islands and Lakes Up North

Chief Wooden Frogs Island, Eagle Island, and **Cemetery Islands** are among the sacred islands that grace **Kabetogama Lake** in Voyageurs National Park. The lake is just over five miles across at its widest point and has a very irregular shoreline. Voyageurs National Park is just outside of International Falls.

Prayer Lake and **Meditation Lake** lie at the northernmost part of Cook County in the Boundary Waters Canoe Area Wilderness. Both are located near the Trails End Campground on the Gunflint Trail (County Highway 12).

Holy Lake is shaped in the form of a cross; it is about 15 miles north of Ely, north of Highway 116.

Ancient Paintings

Human beings today can only speculate about the origin and meaning of rock art left behind by ancient peoples. Northern Minnesota has numerous petroglyphs (designs carved into rock) and pictographs (paintings on rock). The paintings were almost always made with the mineral ochre, also called iron hematite. This substance, sacred to many Native American tribes, bonded directly to the rock, making the paintings virtually permanent. No one knows for sure when the paintings were created—estimates range from a few hundred to a few thousand years ago. And no one knows exactly what they mean, although it is assumed that the designs represent dreams or spiritual beliefs. Some legends claim a water Manitou painted the pictures. Others say that creatures that were half sea lion and half fish painted them.

Explorers first described the pictographs 250 years ago. The red images portray animals (often moose, rabbits, or caribou), medicine men (men with special spiritual abilities), human-made objects such as canoes, and mysterious abstracts that elude definition. The vast majority of images are very small, no larger than a human hand, and appear about five feet above the water line, suggesting that the painters stood in canoes. The largest groupings of these images have been found at Lac La Croix, Irving Island, and the scenic Lady Boot Bay area. Those wanting to see them will have to travel by canoe, because most of the images are located directly over the water.

The most vivid display of pictographs can be found at Hegman Lake, 10 miles north of Ely on the Echo Trail. Many travelers will drive the trail (County Highway 116) from Ely, take a canoe to the pictographs, have lunch and then leave, which makes for a nice day trip. A permit is required to canoe onto the lake and for overnight camping.

More pictographs are located north of Fenske Lake near the Anglework Trail area, Crooked Lake (Lac Croche), Crane Lake along the Ontario Border, the Namakan Narrows, and along the Kawishiwi River about a mile south of Alice Lake.

Petroglyphs at Pipestone National Monument (see chapter 3)

Pipestone Falls and Pipestone Bay

The falls and the bay here are named for the sacred stone at the falls that is used to make peace pipes (see the Pipestone National Monument entry in chapter 3 for more on the sacred significance of pipestone). The site is accessible by canoeing and portaging.

Located three miles southwest of Basswood Lake on the Canadian border, about 20 miles north of Ely.

Height of Land Portage

North Lake and South Lake lie on either side of the Laurentian Divide, with all water south of the divide flowing east and south to Lake Superior and the Atlantic Ocean, and all water north the divide flowing north and west to Hudson Bay and the Arctic Ocean. The Height of Land Portage lies between the two lakes. The site has historic, geographic, and spiritual importance. During the fur-trading era, novice paddlers underwent a ritual in which they were sprinkled with a cedar bough dipped into North Lake and then had to promise they would never kiss a voyageur's wife against her will. They also had to agree never to allow a newcomer to pass the portage without a similar initiation. Following the ceremony, a celebration with shotguns and strong drink was held. Height of Land Portage is accessible by hiking trail, or by canoeing and portaging.

Located in the Boundary Waters Canoe Area Wilderness at the Canadian Border about three miles north of the Gunflint Trail (County Highway 12).

Nanabazoo

According to legend, Nanabazhoo, the great "Pan" of the Ojibwe, smoked dogwood kinnikinnick (a mixture of dried leaves, bark, and tobacco) at Lake Vermillion (Lake "Sunset Glow"), which cuts through 35 miles of the Superior National Forest. The lake encompasses 40,000 acres of water, with 1,200 miles of shoreline. It has 365 scattered islands and is ringed with beautiful granite ledges. It is located in Saint Louis County, near the town of Tower, on Highway 1/169.

Eagle Mountain

At 2,301 feet above sea level, Eagle Mountain is the highest point in Minnesota. From here you can also see the lowest point in the state—Lake Superior, 3.5 miles away, at 602 feet above sea level. A round-trip hike takes about a half a day, and no permit is necessary unless you plan to camp. A plaque near an abandoned logging camp marks the spot of Minnesota's highest point. Migizi, a feathered spirit guide, is said to live there. Try to catch the gorgeous sunset from the top of the mountain—but don't forget to bring a strong flashlight for the trek back down.

Located within the Superior National Forest, with access through Pat Bayle State Forest, 20 miles northwest of Grand Marais at the junction of Forest Roads 153 and 158.

Spirit Island

Located near the Boundary Waters Canoe Area Wilderness, Spirit Island, also known as Picture Island, is set in Nett Lake, among the largest contiguous wild rice beds in the world—8,000 acres. There are about 150 petroglyphs on the island, but permission from the local Bois Forte (from the French for "strong men" or "strength of the woods") Band of Ojibwe is required for visiting. It's on the National Register of Historic Places. The area's only road goes by the Geeday Gah Mi Goong Cemetery.

Located on the Nett Lake Indian Reservation on the border of Koochiching and Saint Louis Counties. For information contact Bois Forte Band of Ojibwe (Nett Lake Community), Nett Lake; (218) 757-3261; www.kstrom.net/isk/maps/mn/nettlake.htm

Spirit Island,
Nett Lake Indian Reservation

Rainy Lake and the Northwestern Border Area

The Rainy Lake area, on the Canadian border near International Falls, is a principal religious gathering place for Cree and Ojibwe Great Indian Medicine Feasts. Historically, both Catholic and Protestant missionaries eventually gave up trying to convert the local "medicine men" from their Midewiwin practices, which involved the use of herbs to promote prolonged life, moderation, and quietness.

Grand Mound

There are about 10,000 burial mounds in Minnesota, primarily in the northern part of the state. There are, however, very few effigy mounds (mounds in the shapes of animals); Wisconsin contains more of these mounds than any other area in the world. Only a few of the original Minnesota mounds remain today, most having been destroyed by the encroachment of western civilization. This desecration is another sad chapter in the nation's treatment of Native Americans. They honored the remains of their loved ones so deeply that nomadic tribes would transport the bones of family members with them to be buried in the area where they were staying.

Minnesota boasts the largest burial mound in the upper Midwest. Grand Mound is set along the banks of the Rainy River, at the junction of the Big Fork River, 17 miles west of International Falls. It is 325 feet around and 25 feet high. The Laurel Indians formed it between 200 B.C.E. and 800 C.E.

The mounds in the area have been excavated and then reconstructed, with repatriation of remains and reinterment through private ceremony by Ojibwe and Dakota elders. In 1884, archaeologists excavated some sections of Grand Mound, and their work left scars on the north and south sides. The other four mounds have had varying degrees of disturbance.

Located at 6749 Highway 11, International Falls, Koochiching County; (218) 285-3332.

Grand Mound Interpretive Center, west of International Falls

McKinstry Mounds

Along with Grand Mound, the McKinstry Mounds near International Falls are all part of the same vast group of mounds located in northern Minnesota and Ontario. Open to the public, the largest of the McKinstry Mounds is 83 feet in diameter and 8.5 feet high. These mounds are connected to the Kay-Nah-Chi-Wah-Nung Mounds (just across the Canadian border in Ontario). The McKinstry Mounds, also known as the Pelland Mounds, are on the National Register of Historic Places. The burials were removed in 1939 and reinterred in another mound at Grand Mound center in 1991.

Located between Grand Mound and International Falls, on Highway 11 at Highway 71 (east of Pelland), in Koochiching County.

Migizi (Eagle) Nests

Sacred to many Native American tribes, eagles have built nests in aspen trees between Highway 11 and the Rainy River. They can be seen between mile markers 163 and 164, between mile markers 168 and 169 by the curve sign, and between mile markers 169 and 170.

The Headwaters Area

White Oak Point

In 1940 and 1954, University of Minnesota professor Lloyd A. Wilford excavated a large prehistoric habitation on the shores of a gradual bend in the Mississippi River. The archaeological evidence, including ancient earthen mounds, that he and others uncovered, spans thousands of years. These excavations and later artifact studies gave archaeologists an index of the Woodland cultural components in the Northern Headwaters Area. Here the river meanders through an extensive marsh, and it is the only tract of high ground within several miles that is directly accessible from the river.

Located on the Mississippi River near the city of Deer River, Itasca County.

Leech Lake Indian Reservation

Long ago, a giant leech was said to have been seen swimming across Leech Lake—hence the name. The reservation that bears the same name spans Cass, Hubbard, Becker, and Clearwater Counties and includes at least 34 cemeteries, burial sites, and prehistoric burial mounds, as well as many other historic sites. Most of the reservation lies within the Chippewa National Forest. Three of Minnesota's larger lakes—Winnibigoshsish and Cass, in addition to Leech—are here, and are all linked by the Mississippi River. In addition, surveys have located 2,800 cultural resource sites within the reservation boundaries.

The Leech Lake Band of Ojibwe and the U.S. Army fought their last battle in the area at Battle Point in 1898. The Ojibwe had long been alienated as a result of unfair law enforcement, illegal timber sales, and other issues. Today, a cultural museum is planned for the site. Since the 1970s, the Chippewa National Forest Heritage Program has worked to manage cultural resources, focusing on federal and state preservation laws and regulations.

For more information, contact the Leech Lake Band of Ojibwe, Cass Lake; (218) 335-8309 (site preservation officer) or (218) 335-2252 (tribal office); www.leechlakeojibwe.org

Lake Windigo

Lake Windigo is actually in the center of an island (Star) that itself is set in a lake (Cass). According to Ojibwe folklore, the Windigo were large ice monsters that wandered in the winter woods hunting people to eat—a village at a time! The Windigo could remove an outer layer of ice and appear human. As a result, newcomers to Ojibwe villages were treated with suspicion until villagers were sure the recent arrivals weren't going to eat them. Windigos could be stopped only with magic, but in human form they could also be speared to death. Some believed a Windigo was an isolated shaman who had gone crazy and become a cannibal. There are similar legends in other cold climates.

Not all believed Windigos was evil. The term means "those that go backwards," and could be applied to tricksters. The few people considered authentic Windigos were held in great respect and seen as extremely powerful.

Located 12 miles southeast of Bemidji on Star Island, within Cass Lake, Chippewa National Forest. For more information, contact the Chippewa National Forest Headquarters, Cass Lake; (218) 335-2226.

Ogema Geshik (Sun Chief) Point

Over the last 3,000 years, up to five different Woodland cultural groups occupied Ogema Geshik Point, which shows evidence of the earliest harvesting of wild rice in the Headwaters Area. The site is located on a peninsula that juts out into the Bowstring River about one mile northwest of Bowstring Lake. In addition to its bountiful wild rice, the point probably contained mounds and a village site. Brainerd, Laurel, Blackduck, Sandy Lake, and Oneota Cultures are believed to have lived here.

Located in central Itasca County, about 20 miles northwest of Grand Rapids. The actual site is on tribal lands on a peninsula in the northwest part of Leech Lake. For more information in visiting the site, contact the Leech Lake Heritage Site Program; (218) 335-8095.

Turtle Oracle Mound, Itasca County

Turtle Oracle Mound

One of very few known intaglios in the world, Dakota carved this turtle into the ground rather than built into a mound in the 1700s after winning a battle against the Ojibwe. Originally, the head and tail of the animal pointed to the enemy (with its body curved into a "C"). The Ojibwe later reversed the direction. A snake mound surrounds the turtle. The site, which has also been used as a council area, is on the National Register of Historic Places.

Located on the Cut Foot Sioux Trail near Squaw Lake, Itasca County, approximately 18 miles northwest of the town of Deer River. There is a marked trail to the mound, with parking on Highway 46. For more information, contact the Leech Lake Reservation, Cass Lake; (218) 335-8309 or Chippewa National Forest Headquarters, Cass Lake; (218) 335-2226.

Lake Itasca

"Here, 1,475 ft above the ocean, the mighty Mississippi begins to flow on its winding way 2,552 miles to the Gulf of Mexico," reads a sign at Lake Itasca. Called the "Source of the Father" (the Mississippi), it is the site of the oldest state park in Minnesota, founded in 1891. At 32,000 acres, it is also one of Minnesota's largest state parks. Here it is possible to walk on stepping stones to cross the Mississippi River, which the Ojibwe called Gichiziibi ("great river") and Misiziibi ("river spread over a large area").

Headwaters of the Mississippi at Itasca State Park

*I look back at what the Mississippi is to me, and it's the giver
of life. Everything is a circle—a circle of life. That river's been around
here for thousands of years, and people have been using it for thousands
of years. And people will continue to use it for the next thousands of years.
As long as we keep that circle, don't try to sever all the spines that go
to it, because the Mississippi is just one part of that web.*
—Jim Jones, Jr., Ojibwe, Leech Lake Pillager Band

Go to Peace Pipe Vista for a magnificent view of the lake. You'll also find the Itasca Burial Mounds at a former Dakota village site near the Headwaters Museum. Also of interest is the Itasca Indian Cemetery, along with a pioneer cemetery. Nearby is Preacher's Grove, a stand of red pine trees more than 250 years old and named for a preachers' convention that camped at this location. From here it's just a short distance to the largest red pine and the largest white pine in Minnesota, both more than 350 years old.

Itasca State Park, in Clearwater County, is located near Highway 71, 21 miles north of Park Rapids; (218) 266-2100.

White Cloud Monument

This monument, erected in 1909 on the White Earth Indian Reservation, honors Ojibwe spiritual leader Chief White Cloud (1828–1898).

Located in the Calvary Catholic Cemetery, one mile south of White Earth, Becker County. For more information, contact the White Earth Ojibwe Tribe, White Earth; (218) 983-3285.

Other Mound Sites

Mahnomen Mounds

The Ojibwe word for wild rice, mahnomen, literally means, "gift from God." Wild rice is a delicacy (meenun) delivered by the spirit (Manitou). Elders conduct an annual preharvest ceremony, gathering a handful of rice from each of the bays and offering it to the water with tobacco and a prayer of thanksgiving. At Mahnomen Mounds, a wildlife trail provides a good view of many burial mounds, estimated to be 7,000 years old. Interpretative signs facilitate a self-guided tour. There is an observation tower at the end of the trail. Located in the Sherburne National Wildlife Refuge, northwest of Zimmerman (18 miles north of the Elk River) on Highway 169.

Warner and Lee Mounds

Three burial mounds reside on this site. The 50-foot wide Warner Mounds are located on a patch of high ground on the bank of the Sand Hill River, and the Lee Mound is on the northern edge of the Small Maple River. Both are in Polk County.

Shell River Mounds

Near Park Rapids and Leech Lake in Hubbard County, Shell River Prehistoric Village and Mound District is on the National Register of Historic Places.

Stumne Mounds at Charles A. Lindberg State Park

This park contains a dozen linear and two conical mounds along the trails that go to Pike Creek. The mounds are on the National Register of Historic Places. Located near Little Falls in Royalton Township, Morrison County.

Gull Lake Mounds

Signs of dual and even triple burials have been found here. The burial grounds were excavated in 1969 at what is now Crow Wing State Park. The mound site is on the National Register of Historic Places.

Fort Flatmouth Mounds

This group of eight linear mounds is located at Cross Lake in Crow Wing County. It is on the National Register of Historic Places.

Malmo Mounds

These middle woodlands mounds are on the National Register of Historic Places. Located in McGrath, Aitkin County.

Lake Traverse Mounds

These excavated burial mounds are near a small village site, near Browns Valley in Traverse County. Near the famous "Browns Valley Man" (the remaining bones of early man in North America) in Big Stone Lake State Park.

The Legend of the Lady's Slipper

According to an Ojibwe legend, there was a young girl who wanted to accompany her older brother on hunting trips, but he would never take her. One day she secretly followed him but became lost in the woods. She couldn't find her brother or the way home. When the family realized she was missing, they started a fire to send smoke signals to help her find her way, but the wind turned and took the fire into the forest, killing the girl. The following spring, pink and white flowers, shaped like moccasins or slippers, sprung up where the girl had walked. Also known as moccasin flower, the lady's slipper's botanical name is cypripedium, Greek for "shoe of Venus." The pink and white lady's slipper is Minnesota's state flower.

Red Lake Reservation

Red Lake is large enough to be seen from space. The Red Lake Band of Ojibwe has lived on land surrounding the lake since the Dakota left in the mid-1700s. A Northwest Fur Company trading post was located at the eastern end of the lake in the early 1800s. Seven chiefs refused to comply with the Land Allotment Act of 1887, which kept the land sovereign to their tribe. Red Lake Reservation is one of only two "closed" reservations in the United States.

To honor the Red Lake Band and to recognize the contributions Native Americans have made to the state, the Minnesota Legislature named Thomas Stillday, Jr., to serve as its official chaplain in 1996. Born in 1934 and raised on the Red Lake Reservation, he was the first religious practitioner outside the Judeo-Christian tradition to serve in that capacity. In accordance with his Native American religious beliefs, there were no photos or recordings of Stillday's opening prayer for the Minnesota Senate in February 1997.

The Narrows, located at Ponemah Point, is the beautiful site of a historic village. About 1,400 parcels of land are scattered throughout Roseau, Lake of the Woods, and Koochiching Counties. Most are in the Northwest Angle, on the northwest edge of Lake of the Woods across from mainland Minnesota.

The Tribal Information Center in Red Lake is open Monday through Friday from 8 a.m. to 4 p.m., with weekend visitation hours upon request.

For more information, contact the Red Lake Band of Ojibwe, Red Lake County; (218) 679-3341; www.redlakenation.org

Ondatamaning

The present town of Redby on the Red Lake Reservation is on the spot where the Indian village of Ondatamaning once stood. Here you can see the grave of the great chief May-Dway-Fwon-No-Nind at Saint Antipas Episcopal Cemetery. Regular powwows were held at the site until the mid-1950s.

Located on Highway 1 along Lower Red Lake.

Old Crossing Treaty Site

The Old Crossing Treaty Site is about 40 miles due west of the Red Lake Reservation. The site is a place of peace where several treaties were signed, including the Grand Council in 1863, when 1,600 Ojibwe and 250 whites negotiated almost two weeks at the site to come up with a peace treaty. As a result, 11 million acres of land were ceded to the United States. The specific site is marked.

Located on the northern bank of the Red Lake River, southwest of Huot on Highway 17.

Mille Lacs Reservation

The Mille Lacs Band of Ojibwe occupy land spread out over Mille Lacs and Aitkin Counties, centering around the lake of the same name. Lake Mille Lacs is the second biggest lake entirely within Minnesota. Its present name comes from the French, who misunderstood the Indian term for "mystic" or "spirit lake" as "thousands of lakes."

In an amusing mistranslation, the "river of good spirits," which flows into Mille Lacs, was renamed the Rum River by the French because rum was the "spirits" they were most familiar with.

Information about the tribe is available from its preservation officer at (320) 532-4209; www.millelacsojibwe.org

Mille Lacs Kathio State Park

The main village of the Mdewakanton Dakota ("people of the spirit lake") once stood at the mouth of the Rum River on the southwestern corner of Lake Mille Lacs. The area, now a national historic landmark, was continually occupied from 3000 B.C. to 1740 A.D. A great battle occurred there in 1745, which changed history; afterward the Dakota went west, and the Ojibwe occupied the land followed by many European settlers. The Kathio Mounds are temple mounds that date back to the Mississippian period. A 100-foot observation tower is open in the summer, and visitors can take a self-guided, interpretive tour of the site.

Mille Lacs Kathio State Park is located several miles northwest of Onamia on Highway 169, along the southwestern shore of Lake Mille Lacs; (320) 532-3523.

Father Hennepin State Park

This park commemorates Father Louis Hennepin, a Jesuit and the first recorded European explorer to visit what is now known as Minnesota. Hennepin was held captive by a war party of 120 Dakota at Lake Mille Lacs in the late 17th century. However, the park is not the site of his capture or release. Albino deer, considered sacred, have been seen in the park. Visitors can see Spirit Rock Island and Hennepin Islands from Pope Point, at the western edge of the park.

Located just off Highway 27, on the southeastern shore of Lake Mille Lacs; (320) 676-8763.

Lake Mille Lacs seen from Father Hennepin State Park

Spirit Rock Island

Mysterious sounds escaping from Lake Mille Lacs, and the fact that Spirit Rock Island appears to move around the lake when the barometric pressure changes, earned it the designation as a "spirit" lake and rock. The island, just off the southwestern shore of Lake Mille Lacs, has no soil but is composed entirely of pink-and-white granite boulders between 15 and 20 feet above the water. Pelicans, gulls, and terns gather there, and the boulders are completely white with bird droppings.

The Dakota regarded boulders as sacred. In addition to painting on the boulders, they also included boulders in their truth-telling oaths, which warned that liars would be punished by falling rocks. Because of the boulders, it's assumed the area has a connection to the Dakota legend of Waziya (or Wayzata), the Winter Man. Also known as the God of the North, he blows the winds of winter from his mouth and nostrils. He is an enemy of I-to-ka-ga Wi-cas-ta (the South Man), and their incessant back-and-forth fighting causes the seasons to change. The South Man is said to have thrown the granite boulders in battle.

Spirit Lake is located about three miles off the southern shore of Lake Mille Lacs.

Mille Lacs Indian Museum

This is considered one of the best Native American museums in the nation. Self-guided hiking paths are located west of the museum, with a focus on man's relationship to the natural world. Call for hours and fees.

Located on Highway 169, two miles north of Mille Lacs Kathio State Park in Vineland; (320) 532-3632; millelacs@mnhs.org

Mikwendaagoziwag Memorial Monument/ Sandy Lake Memorial

The word Mikwendaagoziwag means "they are remembered." This memorial was dedicated in October 2000 to the hundreds of Ojibwe who died of measles and dysentery in the mid-1800s while attempting to remain in their homeland despite the efforts of the federal government to resettle them. They tried to survive on spoiled and inadequate government rations. To build the monument, hundreds of stones (called "grandfathers" and "grandmothers" in the belief that they represent ancestors) were brought from many reservations in Minnesota, Wisconsin, and Michigan. The four colors (red, black, brown, and yellow) represent the four directions and also the four human races. The 19 plaques on display represent the 19 original bands of Ojibwe, and an inner circle of 12 plaques represents the 12 modern bands that are recognized by the federal government. The monument is part of the Sandy Lake Indian Reservation, which was set aside for the band that is part of the Mille Lacs Ojibwe.

Archeological evidence shows human habitation at Big Sandy Lake since the last glaciers retreated, some 10,000 years ago.

Located at the northern end of Big Sandy Lake, north of McGregor, off Highway 65; www.ohwy.com/mn/s/sdylkdam.htm

Other Native American Sites

Wakinyan Site

The legendary dwelling place of Wakinyan, the Thunderbird Chief, is on the far western edge of Minnesota along the South Dakota border. The site features seven boulders with thunderbird signs that look a bit like turkey tracks.

Located in Browns Valley, Traverse County.

$\mathscr{C}$ATHOLIC $\mathscr{S}$ITES

Father Baraga Cross

In 1843, the Reverend Father Frederic Baraga, a Catholic missionary who served the Ojibwe of the upper Midwest, was crossing Lake Superior from

Madeline Island on a small boat when a terrific storm hit. Somehow, he survived, landing near the mouth of a river on Superior's north shore. As a gift to God, he nailed a wooden cross to a stump. Today a marble cross marks the spot, with a prayer of gratitude: "In commemoration of the goodness of Almighty God in granting to the Reverend F. R. Baraga, Missionary, a safe traverse from La Pointe to this place, August 1843." Father Baraga is known as the "Apostle to the Ojibwe." Calling the cross the "wood of the soul," or "disembodied spirit," the Ojibwe named the river Tchibaiatigo zibi, "wood-of-the-soul-or-spirit river." The visitor will find a beautiful waterfall and footpaths along a gorge with a series of cascades.

Located just off Highway 61 at the Cross River, near Schroeder, Cook County.

Saint Francis Xavier Church

Founded by Jesuits and then cared for by the Benedictines, this parish was established in 1895. In the beginning, Father Joseph Sprecht served 100 Ojibwe at the church. The church was part of Chippewa City, a former village. An annual service of mass is held every July 4th, sponsored by Saint John's in Grand Marais. Nearby are beautiful trails that lead to canyons along the Devil Track River.

Located one mile east of Grand Marais on Highway 61.

Our Lady of the Holy Rosary Church

The oldest Catholic parish in Minnesota, Our Lady of the Holy Rosary has served both Native Americans and immigrants since parishioners erected the first chapel, made of cedar bark and deerskin, in 1838. Father Francis Xavier Pierz dedicated the first chapel and also started a mission school here. The congregation built a log chapel in 1851 and the current log building in 1865. The church building is now covered with white clapboard.

Located in Grand Portage, north of Grand Portage National Monument.

Cathedral of Our Lady of the Rosary

This edifice was established as a cathedral by Bishop Thomas Welch in 1957. It replaced Sacred Heart Cathedral (see the following listing) as the seat of the Diocese of Duluth. The new cathedral was preceded by the Holy Rosary School, which was founded in 1923 and staffed by Dominican Sisters based in Springfield, Illinois. The church is on a hill overlooking Lake Superior.

Located at 2846 East Fourth Street (at Wallace Avenue), Duluth;
(218) 728-3646; www.dioceseduluth.org/church/duhr.htm

Cathedral of Our Lady of the Rosary, Duluth

Sacred Heart Cathedral

The first cathedral of the Diocese of Duluth is on the National Register of Historic Places. Its cathedral status has since been replaced by the Cathedral of Our Lady of the Rosary (see previous listing).

Located at 211 and 206 West Fourth Street, Duluth.

Holy Innocents Perpetual Adoration Chapel

This chapel is at the Fourth Street entrance of St. Mary Star of the Sea Catholic Church and features a plaque with an inscription from Matthew 26:40—"Could you not spend one hour with me?"

Located at St. Mary Star of the Sea Catholic Church, 325 East Third Street, Duluth; (218) 733-0218.

Fort Saint Charles

When Magnusson Island was first settled by Europeans, it was the most northwesterly settlement in North America. At the time, the land was a peninsula. Considered one of the most important historic sites in the state, Fort Saint Charles is a reminder of the earliest French Catholic missionary labors that began in 1732 with the arrival of Canadian explorer and fur trader, Pierre Gaultier de Varennes, Sieur de la Verendrye. The fort was in the area that was known as "New France" and was part of the vast Louisiana Territory at the time. Gaultier de Varennes, now known as the "Pathfinder of the West," was drawn to the area because he had heard Native American tales of a great "western sea." The site is considered of national significance archaeologically, and numerous rock islands give the area a rugged beauty.

Gaultier de Varennes also became the first agriculturist in the Midwest by teaching Native Americans how to sow corn and peas. He also attempted to promote peace between the Dakota and the local Native American tribes.

The fort was named Saint Charles in 1732 in honor of the Marquis Charles de Beauharnois, then governor of French Canada, and also in honor of the Jesuit missionary Father Charles Mesaiger. In 1736, having survived through terrible winters and desperate for food, Father Jean Pierre Aulneau, La Verendrye, and their expedition attempted to travel to Michilimackinac for supplies, but were massacred by a band of Dakota. Their heads were later sent to the fort and their remains buried under the altar of Saint Charles Chapel there.

When the fur trade ceased, the fort was abandoned and literally forgotten. Luckily, Father Aulneau had kept a detailed journal of his life and experiences at the fort, and, 150 years later, the Jesuits discovered the journal. After two expeditions, they found the site of the fort and the remains of the martyrs.

The fort, with the chapel as its centerpiece, was restored in 1950 by Minnesota Fourth Degree Knights of Columbus with a memorial altar as a shrine to all Christians, and dedicated on July 4, 1951, by Bishop Francis J. Schenk. The organization's motto is "Patriotism enlightened and informed by religion."

The restored fort is at the exact site of the original log fort and fur trading post, at the top of the Northwest Angle in Angle Inlet on Lake of the Woods. It is one of only three pre-1763 French fort sites found in Minnesota.

The restored fort is located at Angle Inlet in the Northwest Angle State Forest, accessible via Highway 308 through southeastern Manitoba, by boat, or by airplane. The Lake of the Woods County Museum is on First Street and Third Avenue in Baudette. Magnusson Island is accessible by plane or boat only. A number of nearby resorts provide transportation. (218) 634-1200 or (218) 631-3236; www.entreeltd.com/fortStCharles.htm

Father Aulneau Memorial Church/ Saint Mary's Catholic Church

This is the largest log church in the world, with a roof made of 70,999 hand-split cedar shakes. It was dedicated in 1954.

Located at 202 Roberts Avenue NE, Warroad; (218) 386-1178.

Saint Mary's Mission

Catholic missionaries were ministering to Native Americans in the Red Lake area as early as 1842. In 1855, the apparition of a cross was reportedly sighted over the North Woods. Three years later, Saint Mary's Mission was committed to the Red Lake Band of Ojibwe. The mission is open at various times during the day, but tours are also available.

Located on Highway 1 in the town of Red Lake, Beltrami County. Look for the historic plaque near the highway in front of the compound. (218) 679-3614 or (218) 679-3615; www.crookston.org/redlake/missionbeginnings.htm

Church of Saints Joseph and Mary

One of Minnesota's first churches built by and for Ojibwe people, this log structure has a main building and three attached annexes, forming a cross. The original chapel was located inside a wigwam. A newer building next door now contains historic artifacts from the original church, and there is a small cemetery to the north. Nearby are the Mash-ka-wisen Treatment Center and a powwow ring. The site, located on the Fond du Lac Indian Reservation, is on the National Register of Historic Places.

Located on the west side of Big Lake along Mission Road, about five miles west of Cloquet, Carlton County.

Church of Saints Joseph and Mary, near Cloquet

National Shrine of Saint Odilia

Many people attribute their healing, especially of the eyes, to visiting this shrine, named for Saint Odilia, patroness of the blind and afflicted. In about 300 C.E., Saint Odilia and her companions were martyred in Cologne as they traveled from England to the East. She appeared to Brother John Novelan of Eppa in 1287, directing him to find her bones in Germany and take her remains to Belgium, the location of the motherhouse of the Crosier Order (the order of Saint Odilia). The remains were hidden for safety during the French Revolution, and in 1910, they were brought to Onamia, Minnesota, the site of the first community of the Crosier Order. In 1950, Holy Cross Church and Academy was built in honor of Saint Odilia. Her bones are encased here in a marble reliquary.

The Crosier fathers and brothers established this shrine in 1952. Since then, they say, "Saint Odilia has kept a promise to shower a stream of graces upon the Crosier Fathers and upon all those who invoke her aid in their hour of need. Thousands visit annually, many more send in prayer requests. Many attribute healing to the shrine and prayers offered there." Members of the Order will bless water by dipping a relic into it and asking God to give it power against disease. The story of the life and martyrdom of Saint Odilia is told on the beautiful stained-glass windows, manufactured by Robert Pinart and the Rambusch Company of New York.

Visitors are asked to have a Crosier priest or brother accompany them when touring the shrine area.

Located within the Holy Cross Catholic Church and Academy, Highway 27 at Highway 169, Onamia; (320) 532-3103.

Shrine of Saint Odilia at Holy Cross Church, Onamia

Pembina Mission

This mission is in the small village of Nay Tah Waush ("smooth sailing") on the White Earth Indian Reservation. One of the mission's buildings was the area's first post office in the early 1900s. The Pembina mission, which started in 1848, formed the congregation of Saint Michael's Catholic Church in nearby Mahnomen. Saint Anne's parish, which has a small Ojibwe cemetery located in Nay Tah Waush, and Saint Benedict Mission Church, in White Earth, continues to operate on the reservation as the continuation of the original mission.

Saint Benedict Mission is located at 36352 County Highway 21, White Earth; (218) 983-3519.

Replica of Mother Mary Ignatious Haye's cabin, Little Falls

Holy Family Church

In 1852, Father Francis Xavier Pierz, a missionary from the Austro-Hungarian Empire, established a mission for French Canadian fur trappers at Belle Prairie on the Mississippi River, north of Little Falls. The mission developed into Holy Family Parish, the first parish in the Diocese of Saint Cloud, and the Holy Family Church is the oldest Catholic church in central Minnesota.

In 1873, the order of the Missionary Franciscan Sisters of the Immaculate Conception was founded here. The site features a replica of the log cabin of the order's founder, Mother Mary Ignatius Hayes, who lived in the cabin from 1873 until she died in 1894. Several of the logs used in the replica are from the original. A plaque outside the cabin quotes Mother Ignatius: "My principle prayer has been to know the will of God and my only resolution is to do it." The sisters taught in Belle Prairie from 1823 to 1968.

A statue of Saint Francis at the church entrance was dedicated in 2000 to the memory of the Franciscan Sisters. The building was renovated in 2000, and a sesquicentennial celebration was held in August 2002. Centering prayers (which are meant to prepare the individual for the presence of God) are held Fridays at 7 p.m., with Taize prayers (simple, repetitive meditations) the first Friday of each month.

Holy Family Church is located at 18777 Riverwood Drive, Little Falls; (320) 632-5720.

Saint Francis Center

This large complex provides numerous opportunities for religious and spiritual renewal. The centerpiece is the beautiful Sacred Heart Chapel, built in 1943 for the Franciscan Sisters of Little Falls, established in 1898. One can see a Romanesque influence in its pillars, rounded arches, and the symbolism of the stained-glass windows. Tours of the chapel and Saint Francis Convent are available by appointment. Individuals and groups can stay at the retreat center.

Located at 116 Eighth Avenue, Little Falls; (320) 632-2981 or (320) 632-0695.

Saint Francis Center, Little Falls

Our Lady of Lourdes

In 1917, Father John Musial established this congregation for people on the west side of the Mississippi River in Little Falls. The twin domes of the ornate church reflect Polish Catholic architecture. The parishioners dedicated the church building in 1923.

Located at 208 West Broadway, Little Falls; (320) 632-8243; www.ourladyoflourdeschurch.org

Church of Saint Joseph

This Gothic church features a 45-foot ceiling and a 160-foot steeple. Construction was completed in 1902, and it's on the National Register of Historic Places. The church is in the tiny town named after Father Francis Xavier Pierz, the pioneering missionary who founded several churches throughout the area in the mid-19th century.

Located at 68 Main Street, Pierz; (320) 468-6033; www.pierzmn.com/historicalstjos.html

Crow Wing Missions

The geographic center of the state, what is now Crow Wing State Park was the site of a fierce battle between the Dakota and the Ojibwe in 1768. After Allan Morrison established a trading post at the site in 1823, missionaries soon came. Until 1868, it was the northernmost settlement on the Mississippi River. When a railroad station was opened in Brainerd, the village of Crow Wing vanished, leaving only one house, the Clement Beaulieu House, which has been restored.

The village was known more for its saloons than its churches, but nevertheless several mission churches were established in town during the mid-1800s. In 1852, Father Francis Xavier Pierz arrived to set up a mission, which later led to the establishment of the first permanent Catholic parish in Belle Prairie (see the previous listing for Holy Family Parish). Other missions were the Episcopal Church of the Holy Cross and a Lutheran mission overseen by the Reverend Ottmar Cloetter.

Crow Wing State Park has a chapel where Saturday night mass is said, Memorial Day through Labor Day. There is free park admission and free parking for those attending mass. The park features self-guided trails with information about the natural history and rich heritage of the park.

Crow Wing State Park is nine miles south of Brainerd on Highway 371, at the confluence of the Crow Wing and Mississippi Rivers. The chapel is located at 7100 State Park Road SW, Brainerd; (218) 829-8022.

Saint Francis of Assisi Church

The present church structure was built in 1881, which makes it the oldest church building in continuous use in northwestern Minnesota.

Located at 302 Park Avenue, Fisher (midway between Crookston and East Grand Forks), Polk County; (218) 893-2335.

Christ the King Catholic Church

This church, also known as Saint Joseph's, features onion domes, a Gethsemane grotto, and a Black Madonna (a traditional Polish object of worship), as well as a community center. Construction phases were in 1898, 1908, and 1932. Christ the King Catholic Church is on the National Register of Historic Places.

Located at Seventh Street and Main Street (Highway 71), Browerville, Todd County.

Crucifixion scene at Christ the King Catholic Church, Browerville

Roadside Grotto Shrine

This is a good example of a traditional Polish Catholic roadside grotto. Similar shrines can be found in rural Polish communities throughout North America.

Located on Highway 71, south of Wadena, Todd County.

Saint Mary's Rosary Shrine Grotto Garden

This shrine and garden, built in 1907, has roadside grottos and a rosary shrine garden, with a fountain and Stations of the Cross.

Located in Two Inlets (12 miles northwest of Park Rapids), Becker County; (218) 732-4046.

Resurrection Church

Also known as Holy Family, this church was established in 1897 to serve the Slavic Catholic immigrant community on the Iron Range. The building was erected in 1900, designed and constructed by noted church builder, A. F. Wasielewski of Anoka. The structure is on the National Register of Historic Places.
Located at 307 Adams Avenue, Eveleth; (218) 744-3277.

ᔥUTHERAN ᔕITES

Saint Uhro Statue

This site features a statue of the legendary Saint Uhro, patron saint of Finnish vineyard workers. According to legend, when the grape harvest in Finland was threatened by a plaque of grasshoppers, Saint Uhro spoke to them and they disappeared, never to return. On March 16 each year, the local people celebrate with a festival that includes dressing as grasshoppers and drinking grape juice. The statue shows Saint Uhro with a pitchfork, impaling a giant grasshopper. There is also a small museum on the site.

Located on Highway 71 at the southern end of Menahga (eight miles south of Park Rapids), Wadena County.

Statue of Saint Uhro, Menahga

Holy Cross

This Lutheran settlement was named for a wooden cross said to have been erected at a prairie cemetery near Moorhead by Father Geniun, a missionary from Saint Boniface, Canada. The Lutheran mission site was established by 1891 on the border of Holy Cross and Kurtz Townships, and served the Lutherans on the Minnesota side of the Red River in Clay County. No remnants of the early church remain, but the township retains the name Holy Cross. The only Lutheran church in the area now is Hoff Lutheran Church (affiliated with the Evangelical Lutheran Church in America), near Rustad (five miles north of Comstock); (218) 585-4345.

Stavkirke

A stavkirke (Norwegian for "mast church") follows an architectural style that dates back to the end of the eleventh century, during the reign of Saint Olav of Norway. At that time, Christian beliefs were just being introduced in Scandinavia, and the unique architecture blended ancient Norse tradition with the new ways of worship. Stavkirke architectural design is also known for dragon-scale shingles and carved dragonheads at roof peaks, features meant to scare away evil spirits. Other carved protector animals, such as deer, birds, and fish, may be seen along with stylized crosses.

The Stavkirke at the Heritage Hjemkomst Interpretive Center is one of a few stavkirkes in Minnesota. This replica of a 12th-century Norwegian church is on the Hjemkomst ("homecoming") Center grounds. There is also a life-sized, 77-foot replica of a Viking ship built in 1971. In 1982, the ship sailed from Duluth to Bergen, Norway.

Located at the Heritage Hjemkomst Interpretive Center, 202 North First Avenue, Moorhead, Clay County; (218) 299-5511 or 233-5604.

Apostolic Lutheran Church

The sign on this church says "Suomalainen Kirkko," which simply means "Lutheran Church" in Finnish. The structure was built in 1906 on the Vermilion Iron Range to serve the Finnish miners.

Located in Embarrass (20 miles northeast of Virginia), Saint Louis County. For more information, contact the First Apostolic Lutheran Church in Virginia at (218) 749-6416 or the Apostolic Lutheran Church in Gilbert at (218) 749-6369.

Bethlehem Lutheran Church

This Gothic church, with lumber hand-hewn by Swedish church members, was built in 1897 and served as the religious and social center for the community north of Lake Mille Lacs. The interior has stayed much the same as it was a cen-

141

tury ago. The structure is on the National Register of Historic Places.

Located at 300 Oriole Avenue, Askov (seven miles southeast of Aitkin); (218) 927-3935.

West Moe Lutheran Church

West Moe Lutheran Church is named for a parsonage that once stood on the shore of Minister Lake in Douglas County. The church is located less than a mile from the lake on County Highway 7. There is a stunning scenic view of the Norwegian church's spire from the gravel road off County Highway 8.

Located west of I-94/Highway 52, about 10 miles northwest of Alexandria; (320) 524-2210.

Other Historic Lutheran Churches

Lutheran churches are scattered all over northern Minnesota. The following are a few of the highlights:

• **PARK REGION LUTHER COLLEGE**. Established in 1899, this 1917 Romanesque church is a multi-use religious educational building. Also known as Hillcrest Lutheran Academy, it merged with Concordia College. The building is on the National Register of Historic Places. At 715 West Vernon Avenue, Fergus Falls, Otter Tail County.

• **CLEARWATER EVANGELICAL LUTHERAN CHURCH**. This church is on the National Register of Historic Places, but currently sits vacant. On County Highway 10, near Oklee, Red Lake County.

• **STIKLESTAD UNITED LUTHERAN CHURCH**. This 1875 Gothic Norwegian church is on the National Register of Historic Places but is not currently in use. On County Highway 17, near Doran, Wilkin County.

EPISCOPAL SITES

Saint Columba Mission

Although the Episcopal Church does not canonize saints, Enmegahbowh, an Ojibwe-Ottawa who was a Methodist minister and later an Episcopal priest, is regarded as "blessed" and is as close as one can get to Episcopal sainthood.

Born in 1810 to Ottawa parents, Enmegahbowh, whose name means "One Who Stands Before His People," was Christianized as John Johnson in the Rice Lake Band of Ojibwe in Canada. He was a translator at the mission school of the Methodist Episcopal Church, and in 1834 he began working in missions in Sault Ste. Marie, Michigan. Later he moved to Minnesota where he worked among eight Ojibwe bands. After an argument with a white missionary, he was expelled from the Methodist Church, but then became a missionary and deacon at the Episcopal mission at Gull Lake. That mission later moved to the White Earth Reservation, where a log chapel was built in 1868 and the current stone chapel was erected in 1912.

The original Saint Columba Mission was destroyed in the Chief Hole-in-the-Day Uprising. Enmegahbowh and his family escaped, and with about 40 parishioners, he reestablished the mission church in White Earth in 1867. He was ordained a priest by Bishop Henry Benjamin Whipple, the first Episcopal bishop of Minnesota. Enmegahbow died in 1902 and is buried near the mission at White Earth.

Located on County Highway 34, White Earth, Becker County; (218) 473-2424.

Church of Our Savior

This church, built in 1885, is made of aggregate, fieldstone, and half timbers, which results in an unusual, grotto-like appearance. Church of Our Savior is on the National Register of Historic Places.

Located at 113 NE Fourth Street, Little Falls; (320) 632-5731.

Church of the Good Shepherd

The church, the town of Coleraine's oldest, was erected in 1908 to serve mining superintendents and managers at the Oliver Mining Company on the Iron Range. The pine-and-birch-log structure has beautiful stained-glass windows, and the church is on the National Register of Historic Places.

Located at Cole and Olcott Avenues, Coleraine, Itasca County; (218) 326-6431.

Cass Gilbert Churches

Cass Gilbert, Minnesota's best-known architect, designed two of the state's major Episcopal churches: Saint John the Divine in Moorhead and Saint Paul's in Virginia. Gilbert also designed the Minnesota State Capitol building, the Woolworth Building and the U.S. Customs House in New York City, the Supreme Court building in Washington D.C., and the Saint Louis Art Museum. He designed Saint Paul's in 1895, at the same time he was working on the design for the state capitol—a fact discovered during renovation planning in 1997. There are plans to restore Saint Paul's vestry, which has undergone several changes over the years, to Gilbert's original design. Gilbert also served as a consultant on the design of other churches in Minnesota, including a chapel in Lakewood Cemetery in Minneapolis, as well as churches across the country.

Saint John the Divine is located at 120 South Eighth Street, Moorhead, Clay County; (218) 233-0423. Saint Paul's is located at Third Street South and Third Avenue West, Virginia, Saint Louis County; (218) 741-1379.

$\mathscr{E}$ASTERN $\mathscr{O}$RTHODOX $\mathscr{S}$ITES

Saint Nicholas Ukrainian Orthodox Church ("The Caribou Church")

In the last years of the 19th century, Ukrainian settlers flocked to Manitoba, Canada, and northern Minnesota to start a new life. The area's first Ukrainian Orthodox church, Saint Michael's Ukrainian Church, was built in 1899 in Canada's Arbakka District. Today, similar small churches can be found all over Manitoba, where half a million people are of Ukrainian ancestry.

Back then, to accommodate the growing Ukrainian community (the largest in North America at the time), several more Orthodox churches were built in the area. One of these was Saint Nicholas (affectionately known as "the Caribou church") built in the tiny village of Caribou in 1905, just a mile south of the Canadian border.

For years, Orthodox Ukrainians from Manitoba crossed the border to worship at Saint Nicholas without much interference from customs authorities, but in 1930 boundary laws were enforced, and churchgoers had to go through customs or risk arrest. With the majority of its Ukrainian Orthodox worshipers living in Canada, Saint Nicholas has been used only for special services and funerals for many years.

Although few people live near Saint Nicholas Church, it was beautifully renovated in 1974. The interior is original and the grounds are well kept. In 1975, the first Divine Liturgy in 30 years was held there, and people came from throughout the Midwest and Canada. Saint Nicholas is on the National Register of Historic Places.

Located on County Highway 4, Caribou, Kittson County;
www.hobbydog.net/caribou_church.htm

Saints Peter and Paul Russian Orthodox Church

Early Russian settlers who settled in the far northern Minnesota wilderness built this yellow wood-frame church with a double onion dome on its entrance tower. On the National Register of Historic Places, the building is currently vacant.

Located on Highway 65 in Rauch, Koochiching County.

Saint Nicholas Russian Orthodox Church

This black onion-domed church features gold Russian Orthodox (three-bar) crosses on top.

Located at 422 Second Avenue SW, Chisholm, Saint Louis County;
(218) 254-4971; stnicholas@geminidom.com

Other Orthodox churches in northern Minnesota include Malu Gospodja Serbian Orthodox Church, 1129 101st Avenue West, Duluth, (218) 626-1580; and Twelve Holy Apostles Greek Orthodox Church, 632 East Second Street, Duluth, (218) 722-5957.

*O*THER *C*HRISTIAN *S*ITES

Kensington Runestone in the park bearing its name, Kensington

Kensington Runestone

Could Kensington, Minnesota, be the birthplace of America? A plaque at the site claims it is, and while the theory that Vikings actually discovered America in the 1300s has not been proven, neither has it been disproved. The 202-pound Kensington Runestone, discovered in 1898 by Olaf Ohman, is made of greywacke stone and has runes as well as an inscription purportedly engraved in the stone in 1362. Historian Hjalmar Holand translated the runestone and claimed that it recorded a religious expedition by Magnus Erickson, the Catholic ruler of Norway and Sweden in the 14th century, who first traveled to Greenland in search of "fallen" Christians and later continued to North America. The Mandan Indians, known for their light-colored eyes, are said to have resulted from inter-marriage between the Vikings and the Native Americans.

The inscription on the runestone reads; "8 Goths and 22 Norwegians on exploration journey from Vinland over the West. We had camp by 2 skerries one day's journey north from this stone. We were and fished one day. After we came home we found 10 men were red with blood and dead. Ave Maria Save Us from Evil. . . . Have 10 of our party by the sea to look after our ships 14 days journey from this island. Year 1362."

At Cormorant Lake, near the town of Detroit Lakes, three large stones with triangular holes have been cited as proof that the runestone is real; some people believe that the stones could have been used as anchors for the Viking ships.

Some believe the runestone is a hoax, having been created by a local resident a few years before its "discovery." Authentic or not, the original is on display at the Runestone Museum in Alexandria, 15 miles east of Kensington. In addition, the museum has various other runestone-related exhibits. A replica five times larger than the original is on display at Kensington Runestone Park, the original runestone site, in Kensington.

Kensington Runestone Park is located on County Highway 15 between Highways 55 and 27 in Kensington, Douglas County. The Runestone Museum is at 206 Broadway, Alexandria; (320) 763-3160; www.runestonemuseum.org; bigole@rea-alp.com

Maria Chapel at Diamond Lake Cemetery

The quaint Maria Chapel was built in 1889 between Diamond Lake and Ripple Lake, just north of Lake Mille Lacs. The neighboring cemetery was established in 1891. The earliest graves are unmarked. The cemetery is not currently affiliated with any denomination.

Located on County Highway 52 between Diamond and Ripple Lakes, about five miles north of Lake Mille Lacs and two miles east of Highway 169, Aitkin County.

Saint Mark's African Methodist Episcopal Church, Duluth

Saint Mark's African Methodist Episcopal Church

This late Gothic Revival building, erected in 1900 with Tudor Revival detailing, was built not only for the church congregation but also as a center for economic, political, and civil rights discussions for African Americans. Saint Mark's congregation dates back to 1893. The structure, which was the first AME church in Minnesota, is on the National Register of Historic Places. The church has survived for over a century despite the relatively small number of African Americans living in the Duluth area.

Located at 530 North Fifth Avenue East, Duluth.

Isabella Union Chapel

The village of Isabella has a gas station, a warm-weather café, and this tiny nondenominational wooden chapel with an adjacent cemetery.

Located on Highway 1 in Isabella (35 miles southwest of Ely), Lake County.

Crane Lake Chapel

This simple little United Methodist chapel is at the southeastern edge of vast Voyageurs National Park. Built in 1950 by the American Sunday School union, it has been part of the UMC Mobile Ministry (a ministry of a pastor who covers a large territory) since 1966. The chapel has served as the community church for the Crane Lake and Buyck communities.

Located on County Highway 24 near the village of Crane Lake, Saint Louis County; (218) 993-2325.

Chapel on the Lake

This chapel is primarily used for weddings. Tours are available by appointment. A free brochure is available.

Located at 2400 London Road, Duluth; (218) 724-2680 or (800) 444-8120; www.chapelonthelake.com

Wayside Chapel (Little Flower Mission Church)

This tiny stucco church, which doesn't really look like a church, has been a Native American Christian landmark for years.

Located on Highway 169 near Vineland, across from the Mille Lacs Indian Museum at Indian Point; (320) 532-3107 or (320) 532-4346.

"The Chocolate Chip Church"

The Embarrass Evangelical Free Church is fondly called "the chocolate chip church" by local children because the shape and color of the roof make the church look like a giant chocolate chip from a distance. Built in the 1980s, it is patterned after the Norwegian stavkirkes.

Located on County Highway 1, Embarrass (about 30 miles southwest of Ely), Saint Louis County; (218) 984-3402.

Mission Creek

Edmund F. Ely, a Presbyterian layperson, founded an American Society Mission on the banks of what later became known as Mission Creek, near Fond du Lac, on the southwestern edge of Duluth. Established in 1834, the mission ministered to the Ojibwe and was the site of the first school in Saint Louis County. One can still walk the Mission Creek Trail, used by the early mission-aries, although no building remains there.

The 3.5-mile Mission Creek Trail runs along the western edge of Duluth. The trail begins at the end of 131st Avenue West, where there is parking.

*O*THER *S*ITES

B'nai Abraham Synagogue

Bob Zimmerman—who would later be known as Bob Dylan—was one of the members of the small Jewish community that lived on Minnesota's Iron Range. He, along with many other Jews, moved out of the area in the 1950s. The synagogue in Hibbing where Dylan celebrated his bar mitzvah has been turned into an apartment building, and the synagogue in Eveleth has been destroyed. One of the area's last surviving synagogues is B'nai Abraham in Virginia, which has a limited schedule of present-day services because the required minyan (quorum) of 10 Jewish men is rarely met.

B'nai Abraham was built between 1907 and 1909, and it is on the state's list of its 10 most endangered historic properties. The red-brick building was erected on a stone foundation and has stained-glass windows with a mar-bleized texture. The Preservation Alliance of Minnesota is working to protect this unique religious, cultural, and historic site.

Located at 328 South Fifth Street, Virginia, Saint Louis County.

The only other synagogues in the immediate area are the Orthodox Adas Israel Congregation, 302 East Third Street, Duluth, (218) 722-6459; and the Reform Temple Israel, 1602 East Duluth, Duluth, (218) 724-8857, sstevens@kbjrmail.com

Bridge of Peace

Because Chisholm residents emigrated from many different European countries, the residents constructed the Bridge of Peace on the eastern edge of the city in 1976 to celebrate ancestral diversity. The site features a huge display of the flags of the world, with more being added all the time. The goal is to have a total of about 130 flags, one for every free nation. The bridge was rededicated in 1997. Minnesota Ethnic Days, a 12-day festival, is held there annually.

The bridge crosses Longyear Lake and divides Lake Street east and west. Take Highway 73 into Chisholm and turn east on Lake Street. For more information, contact the Chisholm Chamber of Commerce, 327 West Lake Street, Chisholm; (218) 254-3600 or (800) 422-0806; www.chisholmmnchamber.com/history/bridge_of_peace.htm

Baptism River

The Baptism River, which flows into Lake Superior at Tettegouche State Park, may have been named in honor of early Catholic missionaries in the area, to the dousings that may have taken place at the waterfalls along the river, or to later Protestant missionaries. The visitor can take a beautiful walk on a path from the Baptism River rest area, off Highway 61, that leads to a lake bluff overlooking Nipisiquit and Mic Mac Lakes. There are several waterfalls in the area; one, High Falls, has an 80-foot drop—the tallest waterfall in Minnesota.

Tettegouche State Park is on Highway 61, 63 miles northeast of Duluth, Lake County; (218) 226-6365.

Basshenge

Created by Joseph Gustafeste, a bassist with the Chicago Symphony Orchestra, and dedicated by United Church of Christ and Unitarian clergy, Basshenge was built as "sacred space" and as a sculptural monument to "bassists, musicians and all creatures great and small." Gustafeste modeled his creation after Stonehenge, but used 21 basses, of three different designs, made from 3/8-inch steel. Eighteen of the basses are six feet high and the others, in the center, are 10 feet high.

Ten lintels, or crosspieces, connect the tops of the six-foot basses. Seven of them represent the seven virtues (prudence, temperance, justice, fortitude, faith, hope, and love/charity) and the seven deadly sins (covetousness, pride, lust, anger, gluttony, sloth, and greed). A Brotherhood lintel represents the close and interwoven fellowship of musicians of all creeds and colors.

The project is the result of a collaboration between artists, sculptors, musicians, craftspeople, and engineers, as well as funding from Gustafeste and a grant from the Minnesota Arts Council. Basshenge opened on July 4, 2001.

Basshenge consists of two sites: a barn (Basshenge 7) where master classes and concerts take place and the sculpture itself.

Basshenge 7 is located about 40 miles west of International Falls on Highway 11 along the Rainy River, which marks the U.S.-Canada border. The Basshenge sculpture is seven miles farther west on Highway 11, two miles east of Birchdale; www.basshenge.com

Inspiration Peak

This is the second highest peak in northern Minnesota and the highest in the Glacial Leaf Hills. From atop the conical hill, up to 400 feet above its surroundings, you can get a panoramic view of three counties. The hill summit is a 10-minute, easy walk from the parking area. The writer Sinclair Lewis, who worked to protect the peak, named it "Inspiration."

Located on County Highway 38 at County Highway 5, seven miles west of Urbank and 25 miles southeast of Fergus Falls, Otter Tail County.

Veterans Evergreen Memorial Scenic Drive

Geoff Steiner was a Vietnam veteran suffering from alcoholism and depression when he moved to the North Woods. He found his mood began to lift when he started planting trees. Eventually he planted almost 40,000—by himself—in commemoration of the dead and missing of the war. The fruit of his effort can be seen in the stands of trees along 50 miles of State Highway 23 from Duluth to Askov.

Near the southern end of the route stands the Veteran's Memorial Overlook, with a breathtaking view of the Saint Louis River valley. The memorial is considered a place of healing for war veterans. Red signs mark the area. It is part of the National Scenic Highways program, which recognizes the route's beauty, history, and culture.

On Highway 23 between Askov in Pine County and the Fond du Lac area southwest of Duluth.

Isle Royale National Park

This, the largest island in Lake Superior, is legally part of Michigan, but is actually closer to Minnesota. Native Americans called the island "the floating island" and held it in reverence due to the copper nuggets that can be found there, which they called "sun metal." The island has long parallel ridges running northeast and southwest. It is parallel to the Minnesota shore as well as the Keweenaw Peninsula of Michigan, 50 miles to the southeast.

Because the 200-square-mile island is accessible only by boat or plane, and only nonmotorized travel is allowed on the island, it remains isolated and has made a good eco-lab. The Ishpeming (Ojibwe for "heaven") Trail is 6.5 miles from the Ishpeming Fire Tower at Ishpeming Point in the Malone Bay Lakeside Camp.

The park is open from mid-April to October, with full visitor services available from mid-June through Labor Day.

The island can be reached by regular ferry service from Grand Portage, late spring to mid-October.

RETREAT CENTERS AND BIBLE CAMPS

Camp Onomia (ELCA)

Founded in 1949 as an outdoor ministry for the Evangelical Lutheran Church of America, this retreat and camp just south of Lake Mille Lacs is open year round. It is available for ecumenical use. Conference facilities serve up to 350 people in 78+ rooms (only 29 in winter). Reservations must be made one to six weeks in advance. The Dr. Arthur Braun Memorial Chapel is named after the camp's founder, designer, builder, and leader.

Located at 14202 Shakopee Lake Road (County Highway 26), Onamia; (320) 532-3676 or (800) 822-0152; www.onomia.org

Dwelling in the Woods (Tree of Ancient Wisdom)

This independent, not-for-profit hermitage retreat center is funded solely by guest fees and donations. It promotes spiritual growth of all faiths and respects wisdom at the heart of all religions.

Located at 14044 220th Street, McGrath, Aitkin County; (320) 592-3708. From McGrath, take Highway 65 seven miles to County Highway 2, turn east and drive six miles to the center, which is just before the "Trail Xing" sign.

Luther Crest Bible Camp

This Evangelical Lutheran Church in America camp in western Minnesota is dedicated to building Christian faith, character, and leadership. The retreat and conference facilities serve up to 72 men and women, 10 couples, or 200 children in the summer. Call up to one year in advance for reservations.

Located seven miles north of Alexandria along the shore of Lake Carlos, Douglas County; (320) 846-2431; www.luthercrest.org

Lutheran Island Camp

The Lutheran Church Missouri Synod operates this 67-acre campground. The ecumenical center offers various retreats, serving up to 140 people. It features a tree house village as well as an indoor and outdoor chapel.

Located nine miles west of Henning, Otter Tail County, at 45011 230th Street; (218) 583-2905; islandcamp.org

McCabe Renewal Center

This center is committed to those who wish to "journey with others as they seek wholeness and inner peace." Served by a ministry of the Benedictine

Sisters of Saint Scholastica, it features an outdoor labyrinth. It can serve up to 25 day guests and 18 overnight guests.

Located at 2125 Abbotsford Avenue (at Lewis Street), Duluth; (218) 724-7138 or (218) 724-5266; www.duluthbenedictines.org/McCabe.html

Mount Saint Benedict Center

This ecumenical retreat center is owned and operated by the Sisters of Saint Benedict of Crookston. It features two chapels.

Located at 620 Summit Avenue, Crookston, Polk County; (218) 281-3441; www.msb.net; msbcenter@msb.net

Pathways, Inc.

The Evangelical Lutheran Church of America operates three separate camps in Northern Minnesota. Camp Minne-Wa-Kan, (218) 335-6159, is near the village of Cass Lake, on Lake Andrusia. It features two saunas for group use and cabins with private baths and fireplaces. Camp Emmaus, (218) 335-6159, south of Park Rapids about 12 miles, has hotel-quality rooms with housing for 38 as well as dormitory-style rooms for an additional 38 people. Lake of the Woods Bible Camp, (218) 634-2200, near Baudette, offers mostly summer retreats. It is minutes from the Lake of the Woods on the Canadian border. See www.pathwaysbiblecamps.com

Saints Church Eagle Lake Campgrounds

This campground is part of the Community of Christ (Latter-Day Saints).
Located at 17040/3513 County Highway 102 NE, Brainerd; (218) 764-2985.

Sweetgrass Cove

"A retreat for body, mind and spirit," Sweetgrass Cove features a guesthouse and bodywork studio with therapeutic spa services. Traditional Finnish saunas are offered. Rick Anderson, the innkeeper, is a certified massage practitioner and a member of the Grand Portage Band of Ojibwe.

Located at 6880 East Highway 61, Grand Portage; (218) 475-2421 or (866) 475-2421; www.sweetgrasscove.com; info@sweetgrasscove.com

Trout Lake Camp

The Minnesota Baptist Conference operates this ecumenical camp that offers various retreats from May through October. Conference/camping facilities serve up to 325; youth and family camps are also offered.

Located on Trout Lake Drive, Pine River, Cass County; (218) 543-4565; www.troutlakecamp.org; info@TroutLakeCamp.org

$\mathcal{A}$PPENDIX 1

$\mathcal{L}$ISTS OF $\mathcal{S}$ITES BY $\mathcal{R}$ELIGIOUS $\mathcal{C}$ATEGORY

These lists are offered for specific interests and are not intended to be exhaustive. Some of the sites listed are not included in the main section of the book. This was not an oversight, but rather a symptom of limited space. In addition, there may have been problems adequately identifying a site of historic significance due to inaccurate or conflicting source materials.

1. BUDDHIST SITES

Twin Cities Area
1972 Minnesota Zen Center, Minneapolis
1989 Dharma Field Zen Center, Minneapolis
1991 Karma Thegsum Choling Meditation Center, Minneapolis
1995 Wat Lao, Minneapolis
2000 Gyuto Wheel of Dharma Monastery, Columbia Heights
       Chua Phat An Buddhist Temple, Roseville
       Clouds in Water Zen Center, Saint Paul

Southeastern Minnesota
1999 Wat Lao Minnesota, Farmington

2. CATHOLIC SITES

Twin Cities Area
1680 Father Hennepin Stone, Anoka
1840 Saint Peter's Catholic Church, Mendota
1840 Chapel of Saint Paul, Saint Paul
1851 Saint John the Evangelist Church, Little Canada
1854 Assumption Catholic Church, Saint Paul

1854 Saint Genevieve of Paris Church, Centerville
1856 Our Lady of Lourdes Catholic Church, Minneapolis
1857 Saint Mary's Point, Washington County
1865 Saint Hubertus Church, Chanhassen
1873 Convent of the Visitation, Mendota Heights
1880 Saint Luke's Catholic Church, Saint Paul
1887 Church of Saint Agnes, Saint Paul
1887 Saint Martin's-by-the-Lake, Wayzata
1899 Saint Mary of the Lake Church, Plymouth
1903 Saint Maron Catholic Church, Minneapolis
1905 Our Lady of Victory Chapel, College of Saint Catherine, Saint Paul
1913 Saint Constantine Ukrainian Catholic Church, Minneapolis
1914 Basilica of Saint Mary, Minneapolis
1915 Cathedral of Saint Paul, Saint Paul
1918 Chapel of Saint Thomas Aquinas, Saint Paul
1964 Epiphany Fatima Shrine, Coon Rapids
1977 Loyola Retreat Center, Saint Paul

Southeastern Minnesota
1727 Fort Beauharnois Chapel, Frontenac
1842 Saint Felix Catholic Church, Wabasha
1850 Cathedral of the Sacred Heart, Winona
1850 Saint Henry Church, Saint Henry
1857 Saint Wenceslaus Catholic Church, New Prague
1865 Saint Mary's, Mankato
1865 Our Lady of Good Counsel Chapel, Mankato
1866 Church of the Immaculate Conception, Conception
1868 Saint Nicholas Church, Freeburg
1869 Church of the Holy Trinity, Winona
1871 Saint Wenceslaus of Moravia Catholic Church, Owatonna
1871 Saints Peter and Paul Parish, Mankato
1871 Saint Stanislaus Catholic Church, Winona
1877 Assisi Heights, Rochester
1883 Saint Mary's Hospital, Rochester
1891 Villa Maria Retreat Center, Frontenac
1891 Church of Saint Joseph, Owatonna
0000 Franciscan Retreat, Prior Lake

Southwestern Minnesota
1854 Saint James Catholic Church, Jacob's Prairie
1855 Cathedral of Saint Mary, Saint Cloud
1855 Saint Thomas Catholic Church, Jessenland Township
1856 Saint Michael's Catholic Church, Albertville
1856 Saint John's Abbey, Collegeville
1857 Saint Benedict's Monastery, Saint Joseph
1866 Cathedral of the Holy Trinity, New Ulm
1867 Japanese Martyrs Catholic Church, Sleepy Eye

1872 Seven Dolors Church, Albany
1873 Saint Mary, Help of Christians Church, Saint Augusta
1874 Saint Joseph Church, Saint Joseph
1875 Saint Boniface (Saint Mary's), Melrose
1876 Assumption Chapel (the "Grasshopper Chapel"), Cold Spring
1878 Saint Boniface Parish, Cold Spring
1880 Saint Stephen Church, Saint Stephen
1882 Church of the Sacred Heart, Freeport
1886 Saint Mary's Church, Sleepy Eye
1900 Immaculate Conception, Avon/Saint Anna
1904 Way of the Cross, New Ulm
1921 Church of the Sacred Heart, Heron Lake
1952 Christ the King Retreat Center, Buffalo
1972 Schoenstatt Shrine and Retreat Center, Sleepy Eye
1982 Shrine of the Divine Mercy, Sauk Centre
1985 Clare's Well, Annandale

Northern Minnesota
1362 Kensington Runestone, Alexandria
1732 Fort Saint Charles, Magnusson Island
1823 Missionary Franciscan Sisters of the Immaculate, Belle Prairie
1843 Baraga (Cross) River, Schroeder
1848 Pembina Mission, Mahnomen
1852 Crow Wing Missions, Crow Wing State Park
1852 Holy Family Catholic Church, Belle Prairie
1855 Saint Mary's Mission, Red Lake
1865 Our Lady of the Holy Rosary Church, Grand Portage
1881 Saint Francis of Assisi Church, Fisher
1884 Church of Saints Joseph and Mary, Perch Lake
1885 Church of Saint Joseph, Pierz
1895 Saint Francis Xavier Church, Chippewa City (Grand Marais)
1896 Sacred Heart Cathedral, Duluth
1897 Holy Family/Resurrection Church, Eveleth
1898 Christ the King Catholic Church, Browerville
1898 Saint Francis Center, Little Falls
1900 Church of Saints Peter and Paul, Gilman
1902 Saints Peter and Paul Ukrainian Catholic Church, Chisholm
1907 Saint Mary's Rosary Shrine Grotto Garden, Two Inlets
1914 McCabe Renewal Center, Duluth
1917 Our Lady of Lourdes, Little Falls
1922 Mount Saint Benedict Center, Crookston
1952 National Shrine of Saint Odilia, Onamia
1957 Cathedral of Our Lady of the Rosary, Duluth

3. EPISCOPAL SITES

Twin Cities Area
0000 Church of Gethsemane, Minneapolis
1853 Trinity Church, Excelsior
1858 Saint Mark's Cathedral, Minneapolis
1863 Saint Mary's Episcopal Church, Basswood Grove
1883 Christ Episcopal Church, Woodbury

Southeastern Minnesota
1856 All Saints Church, Northfield
1858 Christ Church, Red Wing
1859 Cathedral of Our Merciful Savior, Faribault
1865 Chapel of the Good Shepherd, Faribault
1867 Church of the Redeemer, Cannon Falls
1868 Church of the Transfiguration, Belle Plaine
1869 Church of the Holy Comforter, Caledonia
1871 Advent Church, Farmington
1872 Church of the Good Shepherd, Blue Earth
1900 Grace Memorial Episcopal Church, Wabasha

Southwestern Minnesota
1854 Church of Holy Communion Episcopal, Saint Peter
1862 Christ Chapel, Saint Peter
1862 Saint Cornelia's Episcopal Church, Lower Sioux Indian Reservation
1869 Church of the Good Samaritan, Sauk Centre
1871 Trinity Episcopal Church, Litchfield
1878 Holy Trinity Episcopal, Luverne
1879 Christ Church, Benson
1891 Saint John's Episcopal Church, Morton

Northern Minnesota
1852 Saint Columba Mission, White Earth
1885 Church of Our Savior, Little Falls
1908 Church of the Good Shepherd, Coleraine

4. INDIAN MOUND SITES

To visit a mound is to take a step back to the time when ancient peoples lived off the land in a way we no longer comprehend. For them, the spirit world and the material world were not separate, the way it seems to be for us. For them, the very earth was alive. To be properly reverent, one approaches a mound in silence and sprinkles tobacco while addressing the Great Spirit.

There are over 10,000 burial mounds in Minnesota and the majority is located in northern Minnesota. There are also platform mounds (called temple mounds). There are a few effigy mound sites along the Mississippi River in southeastern Minnesota and northeastern Iowa. Southern Wisconsin has the largest concentration of effigy mounds in the world. For more information on those, see our *Sacred Sites of Wisconsin,* also published by Trails Books.

The following mounds are open to the public. However, some of the exact locations cannot be divulged for protection and privacy. Check the listing in this guide for more information. You'll have to pay a fee if you visit mounds in a state park. When visiting mounds, it's okay to take pictures—just be quiet and respectful (even if there's no one else around).

For more information on laws and agencies pertaining to Indian mounds, read "A Note about the Preservation of Sacred Places (page XV). In addition, the office of the Minnesota state archeologist maintains a Web page, "Distribution of Earthworks and Early Burials in Minnesota" (www.admin.state.mn.us/osa/mnarch/burialmap.html).

Twin Cities Area
Mound Trail, Centerville
Bloomington Ferry Mound Group, Bloomington
Coldwater Spring, Minnehaha State Park
Indian Mounds Park, Saint Paul
Chaska Burial Mounds, Chaska

Southeastern Minnesota
Williams Minneopa Learning Center, Mankato
Red Wing Mounds, Prairie Island
Dakota Burial Mounds, Shakopee
Great River Bluffs State Park, Winona
Silvernale Mounds, Red Wing
Afton Indian Mound, Afton
Lower Grey Cloud Island, Cottage Grove

Southwestern Minnesota
Big Stone Lake Mounds, Big Stone Lake State Park
Upper Sioux Agency Burial Mound, Granite Falls
Minnewaska Burial Mound, Glenwood

Northern Minnesota
Lake Itasca burial mounds, Itasca State Park
Gull Lake Burial Site, Gull Lake
Turtle Oracle Mound, Chippewa National Forest
Grand Mound, Laurel
Laurel Mounds, Laurel
Mahnoman Mounds, Sherburne National Wildlife Refuge
McKinstry Mounds, Pelland
Red River Mounds, Morrison
Warner Mounds, Sand Hill River
Lee Mound, Small Maple River
Morrison Mounds, Morrison County

Shell River Mounds, Shell River
Stumne Mounds, Charles A. Lindberg State Park, Little Falls
Fort Flatmouth Mounds, Cross Lake
Malmo Mounds, McGrath
Kathio Mounds, Mille Lacs Kathio State Park, near Onamia
Lake Traverse Mounds, Brownsville

5. ISLAMIC SITES

Twin Cities Area
Islamic Center of Minnesota, Fridley
Masjid Al-Rahman, Bloomington
Masjid Al-Salaam, Maplewood
Masjid An-Nur, Minneapolis
Masjid At-Taqwa, Saint Paul

Southeastern Minnesota
Dar Abi Bakr Islamic Center, Mankato
Rochester Islamic Center
Islamic Center of Winona

6. JEWISH SITES

Twin Cities Area
1855 Mount Zion Temple, Saint Paul
1878 Temple Israel, Minneapolis
1880 Kenneseth Israel Congregation, Saint Louis Park
1880 Adath Jeshurun Synagogue, Minnetonka
1889 B'Nai Emet Synagogue, Saint Louis Park
1922 Beth El Synagogue, Saint Louis Park
1955 Temple of Aaron Synagogue, Saint Paul
1981 Bet Shalom Congregation, Minnetonka
1985 Beth Jacob Congregation, Mendota Heights
1988 Shir Tikvah Congregation, Minneapolis

Southeastern Minnesota
1910 B'nai Israel Synagogue, Rochester

Northern Minnesota
1907 B'nai Abraham Synagogue, Virginia
1889 Adas Israel Congregation, Duluth

7. LUTHERAN SITES

Twin Cities Area
1843 Norway Lutheran Church/The Old Muskego Church, Saint Paul

1882 Swedish Evangelical Lutheran Church, Ham Lake
1926 Central Lutheran Church, Minneapolis
1949 Christ Church Lutheran, Minneapolis

Southeastern Minnesota
1854 Chisago Lake Lutheran Church, Center City
1855 Vasa Lutheran Church, Vasa
0000 Stone Church, Cross of Christ Lutheran, Houston
1856 Gammelkyrkan, Scandia
1858 Immanuel Lutheran Church, Hay Creek
1859 Hauge Lutheran Church, Kenyon
1860 First Evangelical (Swedish) Lutheran Church, Taylors Falls
1863 Cross of Christ Lutheran Stone Church, Red Wing
1867 Saint Olaf College, Northfield
1867 Fish Lake Lutheran Church, North Branch
1868 Faith Lutheran Church of Black Hammer, Black Hammer
1874 Boe Chapel, Northfield
1878 Den Svenska Evangeliska Lutherska, Forest
1908 Vista Lutheran Church, Otisco Township
1927 Bethany Lutheran College, Mankato
1972 Mount Olivet Retreat Center, Farmington

Southwestern Minnesota
1862 Gustavus Adolphus College, Saint Peter
1862 Norway Lake Lutheran Churches, Norway Lake
1866 East Union Lutheran Church, East Union
1866 Mamre Free Lutheran Church, Mamre
1871 Hawk Creek Evangelical Lutheran Church, Sacred Heart
1872 Kviteseid Lutheran Church, Milan
1873 Beaver Creek Church, Hadley
1877 Zion Lutheran Church, Arlington
1880 Fron Lutheran Church, Starbuck
1881 Westerheim Icelandic Lutheran Church/Saint Paul's Evangelical
       Lutheran Church, Minnesota
1883 Marysville Swedesburg Lutheran Church, Waverly
1884 Martin Luther College, New Ulm
1885 Danebod Lutheran Church, Tyler
1886 First Lutheran Church, Renville
1887 Saint Paul Icelandic Lutheran
1938 Green Lake Lutheran Ministries Bible Camp, Spicer
1946 Shetek Lutheran Ministries Bible Camp, Slayton
1967 Chi Rho Center, Annandale

Northern Minnesota
1861 Holy Cross Settlement, Clay County
1867 West Moe Lutheran Church, Moe
1870 Saint John's Lutheran Church, Bradford Township

1874 Ebenezer Lutheran Church, Leaf Valley
1874 Zion Evangelical Lutheran Church, Chisago City
1875 Svenska Mission Kyrka I Sodre Maple Ridge, Braham
1875 Stiklestad United Lutheran Church, Doran
1875 Clearwater Evangelical Lutheran Church, Oklee
1887 Immanuel Lutheran Church, Almelund
1897 Bethlehem Lutheran Church, Askov
1899 Park Region Luther College, Fergus Falls
1906 Apostolic Lutheran Church, Embarrass
1949 Camp Onomia, Onamia

8. METHODIST SITES

Twin Cities Area
1852 Wesley United Methodist Church, Minneapolis
1914 Hennepin Avenue United Methodist Church, Minneapolis

Southeastern Minnesota
1839 Newport United Methodist Church Log Cabin, Newport
1856 Spring Valley Methodist Episcopal Church, Nerstrand
1856 Lenora Stone United Methodist Church, Lenora
1857 Rice Lake Church, Owatonna
1858 Ottawa Methodist Church, Le Sueur
1861 Taylors Falls United Methodist Church, Taylors Falls
1862 Methodist Episcopal Church, Hastings
1863 Portland Prairie Methodist Episcopal Church, Winona

Southwestern Minnesota
0000 Annandale Methodist Church, Annandale
1858 Simpson Methodist Church, Monticello
1882 Children's Chapel, Walnut Grove
1964 Koinonia Retreat Center, South Haven

Northern Minnesota
1850 Coleraine Methodist Episcopal Church, Coleraine
1890 Saint Mark's African Methodist Episcopal Church, Duluth

9. ORTHODOX CHRISTIAN SITES

Twin Cities Area
1887 Saint Mary's Orthodox Cathedral, Minneapolis
1900 Saint Mary's Greek Orthodox Church, Minneapolis
1913 Saint George Antiochian (Syrian) Orthodox Church, Saint Paul
1913 Saint Mary's Romanian Orthodox Church, Saint Paul
1925 Saint Michael's Ukrainian Orthodox Church, Minneapolis
1936 Ukrainian Orthodox Church of Saint George's, Minneapolis
1957 Saint Panteleimon Russian Orthodox Church, Minneapolis

1963 Saint Mary Coptic Orthodox Church of Minnesota, South Saint Paul
1967 Saint George Greek Orthodox Church, Saint Paul
1988 Russian Orthodox Church of the Resurrection, Fridley
1994 Ethiopian Orthodox Tewahedo Church of Our Savior, Minneapolis
2000 Saint Sahag Armenian Orthodox Church, Saint Paul
2000 Saint Katherine Ukrainian Orthodox Church, Arden Hills

Southwestern Minnesota
1902 Nativity of Holy Mother, Holdingford
2001 Holy Myrrhbearers Orthodox Church in America, Saint Cloud

Northern Minnesota
1905 Saint Nicholas Ukrainian Orthodox Church, Caribou
1915 Saints Peter and Paul Russian Orthodox Church, Rauch

10. PICTOGRAPH AND PETROGLYPH SITES

The list of pictograph and petroglyph sites has been gathered from a variety of sources, but those for the Boundary Waters Canoe Area are based on the work of Michael Furtman in his *Magic On The Rocks: Canoe Country Pictographs* (www.michaelfurtman.com).

Twin Cities Area
Wakon Teebe (Carver's Cave), destroyed

Southeastern Minnesota
Spring Creek Petroglyphs, Red Wing

Southwestern Minnesota
Jeffers Petroglyphs, Cottonwood County
Pipestone National Monument and Three Maidens

Northern Minnesota
Picture Island, Nett Lake
Wakinyan, Brown's Valley

Boundary Waters Canoe Area Wilderness
Basswood River
Burntside Lake
Crooked Lake
Crane Lake
Fenske Lake
Hegman Lakes (three sites)
Island River (two sites)
Kawishiwi River (Fishdance Lake)
Kekekabic Lake
Jordan Lake
Rocky Lake
Sea Gull Lake

11. PRESBYTERIAN AND CONGREGATIONAL SITES

Twin Cities Area
0000 Oak Grove Mission at Lake Calhoun, Minneapolis
1840 Tipi Wa-Kan (Samuel Pond Mission), Shakopee
1849 Oak Grove Presbyterian Church, Bloomington
0000 House of Hope Presbyterian Church, Saint Paul
1855 First Presbyterian Church, Shakopee
1864 First Congregational Church, Cottage Grove
1889 Central Presbyterian, Saint Paul
1897 Westminster Presbyterian Church, Minneapolis
1906 Crane Island, Lake Minnetonka
1909 Stewart Memorial Presbyterian, Minneapolis

Southeastern Minnesota
1849 First Presbyterian Church, Stillwater
1856 First Presbyterian Church, Hastings
1856 First Congregational, Faribault
1856 First Congregational, Zumbrota
1866 Skinner Memorial Chapel, Faribault
1868 Saint Paul's United Church of Christ, Eyota
1879 Peace United Church of Christ, Crooked Creek
1995 Spirit of Life Presbyterian Church, Apple Valley

Southwestern Minnesota
1835 Lac qui Parle Mission, Lac qui Parle
1853 Union Presbyterian Church, Saint Peter
1856 Union Church, Union Grove
1875 Union Congregational Church, Walnut Grove

Northern Minnesota
1891 Barnum Community Church, Barnum
1974 First United Church, Little Falls

*A*PPENDIX 2
*R*ETREAT *C*ENTERS BY *C*OUNTY

The retreat centers listed here may have requirements and/or limitations about the use of their facilities. Some will only accommodate activities related to their religious or spiritual tradition. Others are open to anyone, but have restrictions. Some have few or no restrictions. Please contact the facility before visiting.

TWIN CITIES AREA

Dakota
Convent of the Visitation, Mendota Heights

Ramsey
Christos Center for Spiritual Formation, Lino Lakes
Benedictine Center at Saint Paul's, Saint Paul
Carondelet Center, Saint Paul
Loyola Retreat Center, Saint Paul

Scott
Franciscan Retreat House, Prior Lake

SOUTHEASTERN MINNESOTA

Blue Earth
Our Lady of Good Counsel, Mankato

Chisago
Hazelden Renewal Center, Center City

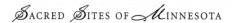

Dakota
Mount Olivet Retreat Center, Farmington

Goodhue
Villa Maria Retreat Center, Frontenac
Dancing Winds Farm, Kenyon

Isanti
ARC Ecumenical Retreat Center, Stanchfield

Le Sueur
Camp Omega, Waterville

Olmsted
Assisi Heights, Rochester

Waseca
Holy Spirit Retreat Center, Janesville

Washington
Jesuit Retreat House, Lake Elmo
Dunrovin, Christian Brothers Retreat Center, Marine-on-Saint-Croix

Winona
Tau Center, Winona

SOUTHWESTERN MINNESOTA

Brown
Schoenstatt Shrine and Retreat Center, Sleepy Eye

Kandiyohi
Green Lake Lutheran Ministries Bible Camp, Spicer

Murray
Shetek Lutheran Ministries Bible Camp, Slayton
Lakota Retreat Center, Slayton

Stearns
Saint John's Abbey, Collegeville
Saint Benedict's Monastery, Saint Joseph

Wright
Chi Rho Center, Annandale
Clare's Well, Annandale
Christ the King Retreat Center, Buffalo
Koinonia Retreat Center, South Haven

NORTHERN MINNESOTA

Aitkin
Dwelling in the Woods, McGrath

Beltrami
Pathways, Inc., Bemidji

Cass
Trout Lake Camp, Pine River

Cook
Cathedral of the Pines, Caribou Lake
Sweetgrass Cove, Grand Portage

Crow Wing
Saints Church Eagle Lake, Brainerd

Douglas
Mount Carmel, Alexandria
Luther Crest Bible Camp, Lake Carlos

Hubbard
Northern Pines Methodist Camp, Park Rapids

Mille Lacs
Camp Onomia, Onamia

Morrison
Linden Hill Conference and Retreat, Little Falls
Saint Francis Center, Little Falls

Otter Tail
Lutheran Island Camp, Henning

Polk
Crookston Mount Saint Benedict Center, Crookston
Shalom Retreat Center, Mentor

Saint Louis
McCabe Renewal Center, Duluth

$\mathscr{S}ELECTED$
$\mathscr{B}IBLIOGRAPHY$

General

• Benson, John. *Transformative Adventures, Vacations and Retreats: An International Directory.* Portland, Ore.: New Millenium Publishing, 1994.

• Bowker, John, ed. *The Oxford Dictionary of World Religions.* London: Oxford University Press, 1997.

• Deemer, Philip, ed. *Ecumenical Directory of Retreat and Conference Centers.* Vol. 1. Boston: Jarrow Press, 1974.

• Devereux, Paul. *Secrets of Ancient and Sacred Sites: The World's Mysterious Heritage.* London: Blandford Press, 1992.

• Harpur, James. *The Atlas of Sacred Places: Meeting Points of Heaven and Earth.* New York: Henry Holt & Company, 1994.

• Hinnels, John R., ed. *A Handbook of Living Religions.* New York: Viking Penguin, 1984.

• Hope, Jane. *The Secret Language of the Soul: A Visual Guide to the Spiritual World.* San Francisco: Chronicle Books, 1997.

• Lethaby, William. *Architecture, Mysticism and Myth.* New York: George Braziller, 1974.

• Morreale, Don. *Buddhist America: Center, Retreats, Practices.* Santa Fe, N. Mex.: John Muir Publications, 1988.

• ———. *The Complete Guide to Buddhist America.* Boston: Shambhala, 1998.

• Wilson, Colin. *Atlas of Holy Places and Sacred Sites: An Illustrated Guide.* New York: DK Publishing, 1996.

• Zirblis, Raymond Paul. *Country Churches.* London: MetroBooks, 1998.

General North America

• Anderson, Arlow W. *The Salt of the Earth: History of Norwegian Danish Methodism in America.* Nashville: Parthenon Press, 1962.

• Chiant, Marilyn J. *America's Religious Architecture: Sacred Places for Every Community.* New York: John Wiley & Sons, 1997.

• Coe, Michael, Dean Snow, and Elizabeth Benson. *Atlas of Ancient America.* New York: Facts on File Inc., 1986.

• *Directory of the Members of the Conference on the Religious Life in the Americas,* 1997.

• Gulley, Rosemary Ellen. *Atlas of the Mysterious in North America.* New York: Facts on File, Inc., 1995.

• Joy, Janet. *A Place Apart: Houses of Prayer and Retreat Centers in North America.* Self Published. 1995.

• Kelly, Jack and Marcia Kelly. *Sanctuaries: A Guide to Lodgings in Monasteries, Abbeys and Retreats in the U.S.* New York: Bell Tower/Harmony Books/Crown Publishers, 1996.

• Peterson, Natasha. Sacred Sites: *A Traveler's Guide to North America's Most Powerful, Mystical Landmarks.* Chicago: Contemporary Books, 1988.

• Thornton, Francis Beauchesne. *Catholic Shrines in the United States and Canada.* New York: Wilfred Funk, 1954.

• Versluis, Arthur. *Sacred Earth: The Spiritual Landscape of Native America.* Rochester, Vt.: Inner Traditions, 1992.

General Midwest

• DeHaan, Vici. *State Parks of the Midwest: America's Heartland.* Boulder, Colo.: Cordillera Press, Johnson Books, 1993.

• Hagen, Jeff. *Steeple Chase.* Duluth, Minn.: Pfeifer-Hamilton, 1997.

• Humeston, Barbara, ed. *Midwest Living: Small-Town Getaways.* Des Moines: Meredith Corporation, 1998.

• Middleton, Pat. *Discover! America's Great River Road: Wisconsin, Iowa, Minnesota, Illinois.* Stoddard, Wis.: Heritage Press, 1991.

• Preus, J. C. K., ed. *Norsemen Found a Church: An Old Heritage in a New Land.* Minneapolis: Augsburg Publishing House, 1953.

• Stumm, Robert. *A Postcard Journey Along the Upper Mississippi.* Springfield, Ill.: Templegate Publishers, 1997.

• Woodhead, Henry, ed. *People of the Lakes.* Richmond, Va.: Time Life Books, 1994.

Minnesota

• Arthur, Anne. *Minnesota's State Parks.* Cambridge, Minn.: Adventure Publications, 1998.

• Blashfield, Jean. *Awesome Almanac—Minnesota.* Fontana, Wis.: B & B Publishing, 1993.

• Blegen, Theodore C. *Minnesota: A History of the State.* Saint Paul: University of Minnesota Press, 1975.

• Breining, Greg. *Minnesota.* Oakland, Calif.: Compass American Guides, 2000.

• Buchanan, James W. *Minnesota Walk Book: A Guide to Backpacking and Hiking.* 4 Vols. Minneapolis: Nodin Press, 1982.

• Davies, Phil. *Scenic Driving Minnesota.* Helena and Billings, Mont.: Falcon Press, 1997.

• *Explore Minnesota 2002 Travel Guide.* Saint Paul: Minnesota Office of Tourism, 2002.

• Hintz, Martin. *Country Roads of Minnesota.* Castine, Maine: Country Roads Press, 1994.

• ———. *Natural Wonders of Minnesota: Exploring Wild and Scenic Places.* 2d ed. Lincolnwood, Ill.: Country Roads Press, 2000.

• Holmquist, June Drenning, and Jean A. Brookins. *Minnesota's Major Historic Sites: A Guide.* Saint Paul: Minnesota Historical Society Press, 1972.

• Johnston, Patricia Condon. *Minnesota: Portrait of the Land and Its People.* Helena, Mont.: American Geographic Publishing, 1987.

• Lass, William. *Minnesota: A History.* New York: W. W. Norton, 1998.

• *Let's Travel Pathways Through Minnesota.* Saint Paul: Clark and Miles Publishing, 1995.

• Lewis, Anne Gillespie. *The Minnesota Guide.* Golden, Colo.: Fulcrum Publishing, 1999.

• *Minnesota Atlas and Gazetteer.* Yarmouth, Maine: DeLorme, 1994.

• Olsenius, Richard. *Minnesota Travel Companion,* Wayzata, Minn.: Bluestem Productions, 1982.

• ———. *Minnesota Travel Companion: A Guide to History Along Minnesota's Highways.* Minneapolis: University of Minnesota Press, 2001.

• Perish, Shawn. *Backroads of Minnesota: Your Guide to Minnesota's Most Scenic Backroad Adventures.* Stillwater, Minn.: Voyaguer Press, 2002.

• Shepard, John G. *Minnesota Backroads.* Helena, Mont.: American Geographic Publishing, 1990.

• Upham, Warren. *Minnesota Place Names: A Geographical Encyclopedia.* Saint Paul: Minnesota Historical Society, 2000.

• Weinberger, Mark. *Minnesota: Off the Beaten Path.* 5th ed. Guilford, Conn.: Globe Pequot, 2001.

• Wood, Douglas. *Minnesota: The Spirit of the Land.* Stillwater, Minn.: Voyageur Press, 1995.

Local Resources

• *Access: Minneapolis/Saint Paul.* New York: HarperCollins, 1998.

• Arthur, Lindsay, and Jean Arthur. *Twin Cities Uncovered.* Plano, Tex.: Seaside Press, Wordware Publishing, 1996.

• Beymer, Robert. *The Boundary Waters Canoe Area.* 6th ed. 2 Vols. Berkeley, Calif.: Wilderness Press, 2000.

• Blegen, Theodore C. *The Kensington Rune Stone: New Light on an Old Riddle.* Saint Paul: Minnesota Historical Society Press, 1968.

• Bolz, J. Arnold. *Portage into the Past. Minneapolis:* University of Minnesota Press, 1960.

• DuFresne, Jim. *Voyageurs National Park: Water Routes, Foot Paths and Ski Trails.* Seattle: The Mountaineers, 1986.

• Duncanson, Michael. *A Paddler's Guide to the Boundary Waters Canoe Area.* Virginia, Minn.: Fisher Company, 1976.

• Furtman, Michael. *Magic on the Rocks: Canoe Country Pictographs.* Duluth, Minn.: Birch Portage Press, 2000.

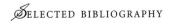
• *God's Name Shall Be Praised From Generation to Generation: Celebrating 125 Years of Ministry in Christ Jesus, 1871–1996.* Sacred Heart, Minn.: Hawk Creek Lutheran Church, 1996.

• Millett, Larry. *Lost Twin Cities.* Saint Paul: Minnesota Historical Society, 1992.

• Nute, Grace Lee. *Rainy River Country: A Brief History of the Region Bordering Minnesota and Ontario.* Saint Paul: Minnesota Historical Society, 1950.

• *Official Visitors' Guide to Minnesota's Twin Cities.* Minneapolis: Minnesota Monthly Publications, 2002.

• Perish, Shawn. *The North Shore: A Four-Season Guide to Minnesota's Favorite Destination.* Duluth, Minn.: Pfeifer-Hamilton, 1992.

• Picharske, David R., and Joseph Amato, eds. *Southwest Minnesota: The Land and the People.* Marshall, Minn.: Crossings Press, 2000.

• *Saint Cloud Minnesota and Central Lakes Area Official 2002 Visitors Guide.* Saint Cloud, Minn.: Saint Cloud Area Convention and Visitors Bureau, 2002.

Selected Web Sites

All the Web sites below were accessed in 2001 and 2002.

• Indian Burial and Sacred Ground Watch,
www.ibsgwatch.imagedjinn.com/action.htm

• Labyrinth Locator, Grace Episcopal Cathedral, San Francisco,
www.gracecathedral.org/labyrinth/newlocator/newdb/

• Minnesota Indian Affairs Council (MIAC), Bemidji,
www.indians.state.mn.us

• Minnesota Historical Society, Saint Paul,
www.mnhs.org

• Minnesota Office of the State Archaeologist, Saint Paul,
www.admin.state.mn.us/osa

• Minnesota Office of Tourism, Saint Paul,
www.exploreminnesota.com

- Minnesota Retreat Center Listings,
  www.findthedivine.com/states/states_mn.html

- Minnesota State Parks, Department of Natural Resources,
  www.dnr.state.mn.us/state_parks

- National Register of Historic Places, U.S. Department of the Interior,
  (Minnesota listings): www.nationalregisterofhistoricplaces.com/MN/state.html

- Partners of Sacred Places, Philadelphia,
  www.sacredplaces.org

- The Pluralism Project: Directory, Harvard University,
  www.pluralism.org/directory

- Sacred Sites International Foundation, Berkeley,
  www.sitesaver.org

- "Windows of the Past," an essay written by Jim Jones, Jr., an Ojibwe,
  www.fromsitetostory.org/stories.asp

NDEX

D

E

MORE GREAT TITLES

FROM TRAILS BOOKS & PRAIRIE OAK PRESS

Activity Guides
- Great Cross-Country Ski Trails: Wisconsin, Minnesota, Michigan & Ontario, Wm. Chad McGrath
- Great Minnesota Walks: 49 Strolls, Rambles, Hikes, and Treks, Wm. Chad McGrath
- Great Wisconsin Walks: 45 Strolls, Rambles, Hikes, and Treks, Wm. Chad McGrath
- Paddling Illinois: 64 Great Trips by Canoe and Kayak, Mike Svob
- Paddling Southern Wisconsin: 82 Great Trips by Canoe and Kayak, Mike Svob
- Paddling Northern Wisconsin: 82 Great Trips by Canoe and Kayak, Mike Svob
- Wisconsin Underground: A Guide to Caves, Mines, and Tunnels in and around the Badger State, Doris Green
- Minnesota Underground & the Best of the Black Hills: A Guide to Mines, Sinks, Caves, and Disappearing Streams, Doris Green

Travel Guides
- Great Little Museums of the Midwest, Christine des Garennes
- Great Minnesota Weekend Adventures, Beth Gauper
- The Great Wisconsin Touring Book: 30 Spectacular Auto Tours, Gary Knowles
- Tastes of Minnesota: A Food Lover's Tour, Donna Tabbert Long
- Wisconsin Lighthouses: A Photographic and Historical Guide, Ken and Barb Wardius
- Wisconsin Waterfalls, Patrick Lisi

- Wisconsin Family Weekends: 20 Fun Trips for You and the Kids,
  Susan Lampert Smith
- County Parks of Wisconsin, Revised Edition, Jeannette and Chet Bell
- Up North Wisconsin: A Region for All Seasons, Sharyn Alden
- Great Wisconsin Taverns: 101 Distinctive Badger Bars, Dennis Boyer
- Great Weekend Adventures, the Editors of Wisconsin Trails
- Eating Well in Wisconsin, Jerry Minnich
- Acorn Guide to Northwest Wisconsin, Tim Bewer

Nature Essays
- Wild Wisconsin Notebook, James Buchholz
- Trout Friends, Bill Stokes
- Northern Passages: Reflections from Lake Superior Country,
  Michael Van Stappen
- River Stories: Growing Up on the Wisconsin, Delores Chamberlain

Home & Garden
- Wisconsin Country Gourmet, Marge Snyder & Suzanne Breckenridge
- Wisconsin Herb Cookbook, Marge Snyder & Suzanne Breckenridge
- Creating a Perennial Garden in the Midwest, Joan Severa
- Wisconsin Garden Guide, Jerry Minnich
- Bountiful Wisconsin: 110 Favorite Recipes, Terese Allen
- Wisconsin's Hometown Flavors, Terese Allen

Historical Books
- Prairie Whistles: Tales of Midwest Railroading, Dennis Boyer
- Barns of Wisconsin, Jerry Apps
- Portrait of the Past: A Photographic Journey Through Wisconsin
  1865-1920, Howard Mead, Jill Dean, and Susan Smith
- Wisconsin: The Story of the Badger State, Norman K. Risjord
- Wisconsin At War: 20th Century Conflicts Through the Eyes of Veterans,
  Dr. James F. McIntosh

Gift Books
- The Spirit of Door County: A Photographic Essay, Darryl R. Beers
- Milwaukee, Photography by Todd Dacquisto
- Duck Hunting on the Fox: Hunting and Decoy-Carving Traditions,
  Stephen M. Miller
- Spirit of the North: A Photographic Journey Through Northern
  Wisconsin, Richard Hamilton Smith

Ghost Stories
- Haunted Wisconsin, Michael Norman and Beth Scott
- W-Files: True Reports of Wisconsin's Unexplained Phenomena, Jay Rath
- The Beast of Bray Road: Tailing Wisconsin's Werewolf, Linda S. Godfrey
- Giants in the Land: Folktales and Legends of Wisconsin, Dennis Boyer

For a free catalog, phone, write, or e-mail us.

Trails Books
P.O. Box 317, Black Earth, WI 53515
(800) 236-8088 • e-mail: books@wistrails.com
www.trailsbooks.com